Rise Up and Build

Neal Pollard

Publishing Designs, Inc.
Huntsville, Alabama

Publishing Designs, Inc.
P. O. Box 3241
Huntsville, Alabama 35810

All Scripture quotation are from the
New American Standard Bible unless
otherwise noted.

Printed in the United States of America

Library of Congress Cataloging-in-Publication Data

Pollard, Neal, 1970—
   Rise up and build / Neal Pollard.
      p. cm.
   Includes bibliographical references.
   ISBN 978-0-929540-62-7 (alk. paper)
   1. Church growth—Biblical teaching. 2. Bible. N.T.—Criticism,
interpretation, etc. I. Title.
   BS2545.C5P65 2007
   253—dc22
                                    2007007851

To Kathy

Having been the recipient
of generous encouragement from so many
in the Lord's church in the work
to which I have dedicated my life,
I have so much for which to be thankful.
Yet, to the one whose encouragement
is most meaningful,
whose efforts are most helpful,
and whose criticisms are most constructive
to the work in which I endeavor,
I adoringly dedicate this volume.
Kathy Pollard is the virtuous woman.
She is smart and funny,
capable and beautiful—
inside and out.
She possesses an endless list of qualities
that heighten the ups
and soften the downs
unique to the preacher.
Never has the proverb rung more true:

"He who finds a wife
finds a good thing
and obtains favor from the Lord"
(Proverbs 18:22).

I know her better than any other.
I respect her more than any other.

Contents

Acknowledgments 7

Introduction 9

1 Expository Exploration 11

2 Evangelism 21

3 Edification 29

4 Education 37

5 Elimination 45

6 Enthusaism 55

7 Eldership 63

8 Effort 71

9 Evangelists 79

10 Encouragement 89

11 Emulation 99

12 Expectation 107

13 Epilogue 115

Additional Resources 119

End Notes 121

Acknowledgments

I am a preacher's kid. I have seen congregations in many different settings, from south Georgia to northern West Virginia. My first love of the church and the work of the preacher came from my parents, Gary and Brenda Pollard. They are two of the Lord's unsung heroes, whose good works only eternity will reveal. Their influence upon me was an unspoken encouragement in the writing of this book.

The one person who has proved most helpful and encouraging during the writing process is Carolyn Elliott, peerless secretary for the Cold Harbor Road Church of Christ. She formatted, edited, punctuated, queried, and generally kept after me to finish this project. Without her efforts, the quality and timeliness of this work would be dubious.

Among the many, many preachers I love and respect, I burdened four men with a request to read my first formal draft. Graciously, Denny Petrillo, David Sain, Wendell Winkler, and William Woodson provided needed guidance, suggestions, and opinions that made a meaningful impact on the final product. Also, I thank the men listed on the back of the book for generous comments after reviewing the finished manuscript. I appreciate the time and expertise all of these men lent.

I am grateful to God for granting me a decade of service with one of the truly great churches among us. In 1994 the Cold Harbor Road Church of Christ took a chance on a 24-year-old boy just two years removed from college. The decision of those elders, Jim Dalton and

Russell Young, has been a supreme blessing to my family and me. Russell has moved to Oklahoma, but the six other bishops since that time under whose oversight we have been—Kieth Fields (now in Georgia), Bill Burton, Derell Ellerbe, Ron Herman, Randy Keeling (now preaching in Marlington, West Virginia), and Dave Young—have helped me develop and mature as a Christian, as well as a gospel preacher. To them and the wonderful families and individuals making up the church family: thank you for your patience, endurance, and kindnesses.

I also count myself privileged beyond description now to serve under the superlative leadership of the Bear Valley Church of Christ in Denver, Colorado, a church that has a history of growth and the potential for phenomenal growth. Harry Denewiler, Mark Hanstein, Sam Kennedy, Clint Stephens, Brian Wilkie, and Maynard Woolley are good, faithful shepherds, and I look forward, God willing, to working with them in building up the church in the West.

Chiefly, I acknowledge my insurmountable debt to God for His grace and His manifold blessings.

INTRODUCTION

- "And all the more believers in the Lord, multitudes of men and women, were constantly added to their number" (Acts 5:14).

- "The word of God kept on spreading; and the number of the disciples continued to increase in Jerusalem" (Acts 6:7).

- "Then had the churches rest throughout all Judea and Galilee and Samaria, and were edified; and walking in the fear of the Lord, and in the comfort of the Holy Spirit, were multiplied" (Acts 9:31).

- "And considerable numbers were brought to the Lord" (Acts 11:24).

There were periods of relief from distress and persecution for the early church (Acts 2:47; 9:31). There were intense periods of struggle, trial, and persecution (Acts 8:1; 9:1–2; 11:19; 12:1–3). In these different circumstances, there was one constant: the church grew! How it grew is of great interest to those of us in the Lord's church today, for every individual and congregation must desire to grow! Numerical growth rarely happens accidentally. Occasionally, a church is the beneficiary of member transfers—Christians relocating, for example. But spiritual growth never happens accidentally. No Christian will ever draw nearer to Christ without making the effort to do so. In the absence of prayer, Bible study, fruit bearing, and active involvement in the works outlined by the Lord in the Bible, members of the church wither and die. In His wrath, God cuts off such people from His fellowship (John 15:2–4).

Every member of the local church is either working for or against her growth. An unfaithful member may argue that he is completely uninvolved, so he cannot be working against the growth of the church. The inactive member—often identified as a "pew sitter," the "Sunday morning only" member, or the "sporadic"—is possibly the greatest deterrent to growth within the congregation. The openly immoral, rebellious Christian leaves no question as to his loyalty. The active, faithful, and godly Christian makes a clear impression as to who his first love is too (cf. Revelation 2:4). The "in betweener," trying to live part time for Satan and part time for the Savior, is the devil's best friend. The uncommitted and those who carry an "I couldn't care less" attitude unravel the fiber that makes for church growth and development.

How wonderful the church would be if each member worked in such a way as to leave behind the spiritual legacy of Stephanas' household, of whom it is said, "It is the firstfruits of Achaia . . . they have addicted themselves to the ministry of the saints" (1 Corinthians 16:15 KJV). The question of relevance is, "Are you addicted to the work of the local church?" How can *you* build up the church of which you are a member? The goal of this book is to build a desire within every Christian member to be both a cause and a contributor to the growth of the local church. To that end, we begin.

CHAPTER ONE

Expository Exploration

Where do we begin our study of the growth of the Lord's church? In the Bible, in those passages that deal directly with its growth. From the very beginning the church was designed to be a living and thriving institution—a growing one. The Bible reveals at least three distinct phases of church growth: the church in prophecy, the church in preparation, and the church in fact. Consider these phases individually.

The Church in Prophecy

Many of the messianic prophesies in the Old Testament are concerned with the fact and the means of establishing God's kingdom. Prophetic passages such as Isaiah 22:2; 27:13; 56:7; and 66:20–24 probably refer to the church. Certainly Isaiah 9:6–7 and Micah 4:1–3 do. However, Isaiah 2:1–4 and Daniel 2:36–44 seem to capture the essence of all Old Testament prophecy concerning the coming church. While God intended these passages to prepare His people for the Christian Age, most of the Jews remained spiritually blind, deaf, and ignorant of their meaning (Matthew 13:13).

Here is Isaiah's description of a coming spiritual city, given about seven hundred years before the event occurred:

> The word which Isaiah the son of Amoz saw concerning Judah and Jerusalem. Now it will come about that in

the last days the mountain of the house of the Lord will be established as the chief of the mountains, and will be raised above the hills; and all the nations will stream to it. And many peoples will come and say, "Come, let us go up to the mountain of the Lord, to the house of the God of Jacob; that He may teach us concerning His ways and that we may walk in His paths." For the law will go forth from Zion and the word of the Lord from Jerusalem. And He will judge between the nations, and will render decisions for many peoples; and they will hammer their swords into plowshares and their spears into pruning hooks. Nation will not lift up sword against nation, and never again will they learn war (Isaiah 2:1–4).

In this brief passage Isaiah sets forth some important characteristics of the coming kingdom:

- *Establishment (v. 2).* The kingdom will not continue only in the mind of God. It will have an earthly presence "in the last days"; that is, at some time after Isaiah's prophecy.

- *Exaltation (v. 2).* The kingdom will "be raised above the hills." Since it is to be the "house of the Lord,"[1] it has to be of the highest quality, an outstanding, notable institution, having no peers among earthly kingdoms.

- *Expansion (vv. 2–3).* The citizens of the kingdom will be from among all nations. Contrasted with the covenant from which other nations were estranged, the covenant under which Isaiah lived (Ephesians 2:12), this coming house is for all those of every race.

---

1. "House of the Lord," does not refer to a literal physical structure or edifice. It is a figurative reference to the household or family of God (cf. 1 Timothy 3:15). Thus, in mind here is the totality of the church—from its Originator and Purchaser to those who gain entrance thereinto according to predetermined conditions.

- *Excitement (v. 3).* Not only will people of all nation-alities and cultures want to be citizens of the proph-esied kingdom, they will also want others to be a part of it. They will invite others to come into this house. No, the coming kingdom will not be titillat-ing to the senses or appealing to fleshly appetites. The excitement is going to be genuine, built upon hope for the future and peace in the present.

- *Evangelism (v. 3).* Citizens will encourage others to join with them in entering and serving God in this house. Isaiah's words imply that others will be called as co-laborers in this great house of the Lord. That citizens will not invite others into the house is not even considered.

- *Education (v. 3).* Within the auspices of this house, the Lord will "teach . . . concerning His ways . . . that we may walk in His paths." This house is go-ing be governed by His teachings (John 12:47–48; Matthew 17:5). Citizens will be expected to "grow in the grace and knowledge of . . . Jesus Christ" (2 Peter 3:18).

- *Administrator (v. 4).* The Lord will be the judge and the lawgiver; He will "render decisions for many people." He is going to be the head of the new king-dom (Ephesians 1:22–23).

- *Influence (v. 4).* Finally, the kingdom of Isaiah's vi-sion will initiate change. The influence of the Lord and His house will transform human lives. It will turn around the hearts of men once set on iniquity. It will bring peace with God to all who flow into it (Romans 5:1), but it will result in the reconcilia-tion of those at odds with one another (Matthew 5:23–24). The church brings together people of diverse backgrounds, including those who were enemies before their conversion. So on the basis of the word of the Lord, this coming house will bring harmonious, mutual acceptance.

A New Kingdom Foretold

While Daniel was in captivity, God gave him the ability to interpret dreams and visions. That is the background of Daniel 2:36–44, which tells us of Nebuchadnezzar's dream in which he saw a great statue. According to Daniel's interpretation, the king foresaw four successive empires: Babylon, Medo-Persian, Greek, and Roman. In the days of the Roman Empire, another unusual kingdom that will outshine all others was to be set up.

Daniel saw God as the architect and builder of that spiritual kingdom (Matthew 16:17–19; Colossians 4:11; 1 Thessalonians 2:12). Since God wanted this kingdom to exist, He effected its establishment. He put His character and seal upon it, distinguishing it from every rival (Matthew 15:13).

By virtue of its divine origin, that new kingdom was to be indestructible; it would stand forever. God would give the blueprints required to establish local organizations of that spiritual kingdom anywhere in the world.

It Shall Stand

That kingdom was established on earth about five hundred years after Daniel's prophecy. Now, two millennia after its establishment, that kingdom still stands, and it will stand until Jesus hands it over to His Father at the end (1 Corinthians 15:24).

The new kingdom is powerful. Again, having the foundational attribute of divine involvement in its formation, this spiritual kingdom is unparalleled in power. Its message, the gospel, is the power of God to salvation (Romans 1:16). Its central act, the cross, provides that power (1 Corinthians 1:18). Its eternal hope, the resurrection of Christ, also provides power for salvation (Philippians 3:10). The rock of God's all-encompassing power serves as the immutable foundation for the gospel, the cross, and the resurrection. Note David's praise to God:

> Blessed are You, O Lord God of Israel our father, forever and ever. Yours, O Lord, is the greatness and the power and the glory and the victory and the majesty, indeed everything that is in the heavens and the earth; Yours is the dominion, O Lord, and You exalt Yourself as head over all (1 Chronicles 29:10–11).

David's majestic language had been rehearsed by God's people for centuries, so the Jews should have been looking for the new house described by Isaiah. They should have been readying themselves for the new kingdom described by Daniel. The few who were ready listened attentively to the teachings of John, an eccentric wilderness man, and his amazing cousin Jesus. Eventually, they began to see Jesus as the person of prophecy. Their faith was forged by hearing the word of God (Romans 10:17).

The Church Explained (Parables)

Nicodemus told Jesus: "Rabbi, we know that You have come from God *as* a teacher; for no one can do these signs that You do unless God is with him" (John 3:2). Nicodemus, along with many others, accepted Jesus' teaching because of the miracles. The multitudes who heard Him deliver the *Sermon on the Mount* "were amazed at His teaching; for He was teaching them as one having authority, and not as their scribes" (Matthew 7:28–29). They accepted His teaching because of its confidence and conviction. Yet even His enemies were confounded, if not

persuaded, by His parables. He also silenced them with
His teaching (Matthew 22:46).

> All these things Jesus spoke to the crowds in parables,
> and He did not speak to them without a parable. This
> was to fulfill what was spoken through the prophet: "I
> will open My mouth in parables; I will utter things hid-
> den since the foundation of the world" (Matthew
> 13:34–35).

Jesus used the parables to teach spiritual truths,
many of which before were locked away in the mind of
God, unrevealed. Jesus used the parables persistently,
telling stories to illustrate powerful spiritual truths. One
of His favorite subjects was that spoken before by Daniel.
About a dozen of the recorded parables begin with Jesus
saying, "The kingdom of heaven is like . . ." So He identified with parables His soon-to-come institution, its like-
nesses and its functions (cf. Mark 1:15).

Here are some of the characteristics of that promised kingdom:

- Will be comprised of people with at least three types
  of hearts (Matthew 13:19–23).

- Will encounter opposition, both from without and
  within (Matthew 13:24–30, 37–40).

- Will experience tremendous growth (Matthew
  13:31–32).

- Will wield great influence upon the world (Matthew 13:33).

- Will be of great value (Matthew 13:44).

- Will be precious (Matthew 13:45–46).

- Will gather every kind (Matthew 13:47–50).

- Will demonstrate greatness through its service
  (Matthew 20:25–28).

- Will demand individual accountability for emulating the compassion and forgiveness they each had received (Matthew 18:23–35).

- Will always be open, so long as opportunity prevails (Matthew 20:1–16).

- Will be harmed by indifference and lack of cooperation (Matthew 22:1–14).

The basic thrust of the kingdom parables is to depict an institution with tremendous life-changing potential. Not only does the kingdom change those who are converted, but it also offers hope and forgiveness to a lost world. That kingdom changed the ancient world, and it has changed forever the lives of countless people. Jesus repeatedly sought to explain to His students the purpose and nature of the coming church. He also warned about the enemies of the kingdom—the devil, the world, the hypocrite, the apathetic, the uncommitted, the worldly, and the unforgiving. He warned about the harm to come from citizens not serving faithfully in the kingdom. Through His tenure as a teacher among men, Jesus set the stage for what the church came to be.

The Church Established (Pentecost Forward)

Many have shown that the teachings and parables of Christ make *kingdom* and *church* synonymous terms in most New Testament references (Matthew 16:18–19). At the time of Christ's ministry, the kingdom was "at hand" (Mark 1:15). It was to come with power in the lifetime of many of Jesus' hearers (Mark 9:1). Following His death, burial, and resurrection Jesus spent much time teaching His disciples about the kingdom of heaven (Acts 1:3). Soon after His ascension, while the apostles were still in Jerusalem, the power came upon them—the power He had promised (Acts 1:8; 2:1–4). Beginning on Pente-

cost, the apostles began to preach the things pertaining
to the kingdom of God (Acts 2:14–40; 8:12; 14:22; 19:8;
20:25; 28:23). Church growth resulted! What Daniel foresaw, Peter and the apostles fulfilled (Acts 2). The conversion of about three thousand honest Jews resulted from
the first gospel sermon (Acts 2:41). God placed them in
the *ekklesia,* that collection of called-out people.

From Pentecost forward, that organized, unified
group held together by the doctrine of Christ as revealed
to His prophetic writers and teachers (2 Thessalonians
2:15; 1 Corinthians 2:12–16), continued to build "on the
foundation of the apostles and prophets, Christ Jesus
Himself being the corner stone, in whom the whole building, being fitted together, is growing into a holy temple
in the Lord" (Ephesians 2:20–21). A thorough study of
the short epistle to the Ephesians clearly demonstrates
that the object of Paul's discussion is the church. The
members of the church were given marching orders
through the epistles. They were called to live holy, distinct lives (James 1:27), to shed light into the spiritual
darkness of those lost in sin (1 Peter 2:9), to meet needs
(Galatians 6:10; James 1:27), to bear the fruit of the Spirit
(Galatians 5:22–23), and to be a general influence for
good wherever they were by living out the teachings of
Christ (Matthew 5:13–16).

Growth Was Not Automatic

Even a casual reading of the New Testament reveals
that church growth did not automatically occur. It was
hindered by sin and beset by eventual decline. The church
in Ephesus started strongly, but that strength soon began to fade (Acts 18:19; 20:17–31; 1 Timothy 1:3; Revelation 2:1–7). Congregations in Corinth, Laodicea, Galatia,
and other places were distracted from their mission by
various sins (1 Corinthians 1:10; Revelation 3:14–17;

Galatians 1:6–9; 3:1). Persecution tempted Christians to withdraw their support from the church's mission.

Yet the evidence of Acts indicates congregations often did enact the gospel in their lives (Acts 2:41; 4:4; 6:1, 7; 9:31; 11:21; 16:5). Consequently, the church grew. Every Bible student knows growth was God's intention, even before the establishment of the church. God wanted His people to reach out to all men everywhere (Acts 2:39–40; 10:34–35; 17:30–31; 1 Timothy 2:4; 2 Peter 3:9). Epistolary writings urged the church to keep growing and reaching out to others (Colossians 1:23; 2 Peter 3:18; 2 Timothy 2:2; Jude 22–23). The congregations addressed, to varying degrees, responded to the challenge. Churches like Jerusalem grew early. Churches like Antioch soon soared in their growth and ability to function as fully mature, effective congregations (Acts 11:23–26; 14:26). In their success, they are a model for modern churches of Christ, as present-day Christians strive to build up the local church.

The *Great Commission* of Jesus has never been rescinded (Mark 16:15–16). The functions of the church have always been to reach the lost, edify the members, oppose Satan, and exercise vigilance over the flock. Having left us records of the acts of early churches, the New Testament provides models of God's desire for church growth.

QUESTIONS FOR THOUGHT

1. How do you account for the growth of the first-century church in both favorable and unfavorable circumstances?

2. Describe the average first-century church member in detail, giving circumstances, backgrounds, and level of involvement in the church.

3. Read Isaiah 2:1–4 and list some surprising prophecies about the church. How did God intend for the church to relate to His overall plan for man?

4. In the kingdom passages of the Gospels, Jesus referenced not only the primacy of God's will in our lives but also the importance of the coming church. List some ways to put God's will first in our lives, and show how they will help the church to grow.

5. Relate an example of public sin in the church. How did the church deal with it? Where are New Testament examples of churches ignoring sin? What has always been the result of dealing scripturally with sin?

CHAPTER TWO

Evangelism

Swelling Versus Growing

One of the flaws of the denominational approach to church growth is the coronation of culture and individual desire as supreme above all else, including the Bible. And our brethren are not innocent in this culture worship. As a result of non-demanding, easy-listening preaching, sensually appealing worship, and offense-free teaching curriculums regarding daily living and denominationalism, congregations sometimes swell in number. Then after a few years, the thrill of worldly religion often wears off. Family by family, the shallow and uncommitted, sometimes in droves, return to what they already had before they became a part of the new and hollow religion.

Yet, Christ's suffering and death on the cross proved it is vital to focus on people (Hebrews 13:12). Almost everyone we meet in our daily routine is lost (Matthew 7:13). And we Christians have the lifeline the world so desperately, if unwittingly, needs! God intended that the saving gospel message be told by the apostles to all whom they contacted, and then that it be further spread throughout the world by those converted as a result (2 Timothy 2:2). The faithful men to be entrusted with the gospel were individual members of local churches.

Needed—Good News!

The gospel is good news in a world sorely in need of good news. A husband and wife sat at the table reading the morning paper when the wife moaned, "Everything I'm reading is violence, immorality, deception, and graft!" The husband, planning to console his wife about the reality of society, looked down at his section of the paper and says, "But, sweetheart, I have the front section. Where are you reading about all these devastating things?" She said, "The comic strips!"

Well, maybe that is an exaggeration, but sin is bad news. It is a weight (Hebrews 12:1), a major cause of heartache and grief (Psalm 31:10), and a destroyer and separator (Ecclesiastes 9:18; Isaiah 59:1–2). The gospel is the remedy for all these spiritual ailments; the world needs an antidote for the devil's poison (1 Peter 5:8).

How Evangelism Builds the Local Church

- *Evangelism is the obedient response to the* Great Commission. The mandates (commands) of the *Great Commission* in Mark 16:15 and Matthew 28:19–20 are to preach and make disciples. Obviously, no one can be—or should they be—forced to accept the good news; the reception to the gospel is both individual and voluntary (Mark 8:34). Yet, the Lord's church should always be doing what God has commanded. Preaching from the pulpit is the Lord's plan for propagating truth in the worship assembly (Acts 2:42; 20:7; 1 Corinthians 1:21). However, the New Testament also reveals individual Christians communicating the gospel of Christ in their daily activities with friends and business associates (Acts 8:4; 11:19; 15:35; Titus 1:3).

- Making disciples, unlike preaching, is a process rather than a single act. By engaging in ongoing studies with prospects—candidates for conversion—Christians are working toward fulfilling the second part of the *Great Commission*. If conversion takes place, a part of evangelizing remains to be done. Matthew 28:20 teaches the necessity of continuing the work by maturing new Christians through further teaching of the whole counsel of God. The objective is stated clearly by passages such as 1 Peter 2:1–2 and Hebrews 5:12–14.

- *Evangelism builds enthusiasm.* Congregations are edified through evangelism. There is an unmistakable air of enthusiasm breathed in by the local church when it is actively participating in soul winning. Hope grows within Christians as they see the church becoming a greater force for good in the community. Community members begin to have a greater awareness of the Lord's church. Positive response to the gospel message of Christ by lost souls reaffirms the faith of those who have already obeyed Christ. Zeal within the local church is contagious (2 Corinthians 9:2). No zeal pleases God more than that insatiable desire to continue to do His will (Titus 2:14). Enthusiasm inevitably begets more enthusiasm. More souls are reached and the local church is edified spiritually and numerically!

- *Evangelism is an active way to fight Satan.* Satan is every Christian's adversary (1 Peter 5:8). He is the enemy of every soul, for he seeks to separate everyone from Christ and the hope of heaven (Hebrews 2:14; Revelation 12:9). No positive trait portrays him. He is completely wicked and supports everything vile, depraved, perverted, and unwholesome. He must be combated. Evangelism is God's plan to fight him, and fight him we must! (Ephesians 6:10–20). Every soul won to Christ threatens Satan's domain. Every soul nurtured and admonished, who subsequently dies in a saved condition, delivers a mighty blow against the father of lies.

- *Evangelism is a basic building block of the local church.* If the church is not engaged in soul winning, the lost die without the hope, joy, and peace that attends the Christian life. Without soul winning, the local church fails to obey God. Without soul winning, the community is deprived of a living, active, and faithful congregation of the New Testament church. Remember the words of Jesus: "Do you not say, 'There are yet four months, and then comes the harvest'? Behold, I say to you, lift up your eyes, and look on the fields, that they are white for harvest" (John 4:35).

CONVERSION[2]

Except a man be born again,
In heaven's kingdom he cannot stand.
Until one puts away all of his sin,
He has no hope for the heavenly land.

Yes by water, but by water, any
Must submit in faithful obedience
To erase the defilement faced by the many
Who refuse God's gracious recompense.

By incorruptible seed one is spiritually reborn
From death of his spirit to new life.
The ever abiding Word one cannot scorn
Nor refuse the Lord's church, Christ's dear wife.

So, come, freely come to the blood of the Lord
For by the gospel He calls you today . . .
And spotless you'll be as His grace He'll afford
Change your course by His Son, the true Way!

---

2. All poems, unless otherwise noted, are written by the author, Neal Pollard.

MAKING IT PRACTICAL

Soul winning is often as simple as broaching the subject with a friend or even a casual acquaintance. A preacher once remarked to a bank teller as he made his deposit: "I have been praying to God for an opportunity to study the Bible with someone. Would you be willing to study?" The woman tearfully replied, "I have been praying for someone to help me understand the Bible better."

This true story may illustrate the providence of God through our obedience to the *Great Commission.* It also serves as a warning. Many Christians are letting golden opportunities pass that could result in saved souls. We often vaguely pray for opportunities to reach the lost and then turn a blind eye to His answer.

Here are some suggestions for making evangelism practical:

- *Have an ongoing training course in evangelism.* Teach a variety of methods, such as *Fishers of Men, Open Bible Study, Jule Miller Video Series,* Robert Oglesby's *One Story,* and the like. Individual Christians vary in their choices of methods according to their personality and knowledge. In a similar way, individual prospects respond differently to different approaches. The average person nowadays knows less about the Bible than the average person of the previous generation did. Some students will be able to read and comprehend well, while others will not have good literacy skills. Teacher preference and prospect interest determine the approach we take and the results that follow.

- *Make evangelism a congregational emphasis.* Encourage the preacher to deliver sermons that instruct and motivate Christians to involve themselves daily in the work of the *Great Commission.*

Encourage the elders to stand regularly before the congregation and pray for the lost and for success in soul winning.

- Conduct soul-saving campaigns in the community. While cold-contact studies are not as fruitful as warm-contact studies, they still serve several purposes. When Christians communicate the gospel to anyone in the proper spirit, that communication leads the teacher to greater maturity and an increased desire to do God's work. Honest souls, many of whom are cold contacts, are in your community searching for truth. Campaigns are tantamount to free advertising; they demonstrate to the community that the church is not only present but that it is also active and committed.

- *Focus on leading souls to Christ.* Encourage the congregation to set quarterly goals for conversions. Even if the target number is enthusiastically high, it will likely lead a congregation to exceed its normal number of baptisms. A tangible figure often serves as a beacon and causes the church to become goal oriented.

- *Involve one-talent Christians in evangelism.* Think of all the peripheral needs of a Bible study: babysitters for prospects or teachers engaged in studies, assemblies to pray for the studies in progress, workers to hang tracts and information about the church on doors, Christians to invite these dear, lost ones into their homes for meals or desserts, record keepers to track the studies and their progress, and many more.

- *Use experts to motivate the church.* Invite personal evangelists—experts in sound, biblical, and proven church growth methods—to teach and train the congregation in more effective ways of evangelism. That investment will pay great dividends. Speakers not known to the congregation will generate special interest, bring fresh ideas, and motivate reluctant Christians in a manner that local talent will not.

Questions for Thought

1. How does embracing denominationalism or considering the church of Christ a denomination hinder evangelism?

2. What are some of the most difficult barriers to overcome in order to evangelize effectively? What are some temptations we face when attempting to win souls?

3. What are the results of evangelism being left to only a few—elders, preachers, or one or two "interested members"? What can be done to involve more members in soul winning?

4. In addition to setting up and conducting studies, what are some ways Christians can be involved in the soul-winning process.

5. Consider the following premise: Satan rejoices when churches have no interest in soul winning. Is it true or false? Defend your answer.

CHAPTER THREE

Edification

A Byproduct of Spiritual Health

Spoken to the Rome church by the inspired Paul, written to church members by a church member about church members, and consequently for every Christian today, Romans 14:19 says, "So then we pursue the things which make for peace and the building up of one another." Edifying—building up—the church has always been a primary principle with God (1 Corinthians 14:12). Edification is a natural byproduct of a spiritually healthy, obedient congregation (Ephesians 4:11–12).

If the answer to maintaining unity and love within a congregation were reduced to one word, perhaps the word would be *edify*. By definition, *edify* means "to promote growth in Christian wisdom, affection, grace, virtue, holiness, blessedness." Edification is actually living out the *Golden Rule* as we deal with our spiritual family (Matthew 7:12). Imitating the behavior of Christ should compel us, His disciples, to be concerned deeply with the spiritual welfare of other saints and motivate us to encourage their spiritual growth.

The Bible teaches that the church grows by means of edification. From passages that deal with church growth, we can learn how we can contribute to the spiritual growth of other Christians. Let's examine how edification is achieved through worship, preaching, and association.

Edification through Worship

Hebrews 10:25 explicitly addresses the subject of mandatory regular assemblies for Christians. In that verse, the most important word may be *but*. That little conjunction contrasts the discouraging effect of willfully forsaking brethren with the constructive impact made by faithful attendees. The first half of the verse forbids forsaking the assembly. The second half of the verse positively admonishes Christians to be "exhorting one another: and so much the more, as ye see the day approaching" (KJV). *Exhort* simply means "to encourage and entreat," and that exhortation is to be done in view of a specific day—not Sunday, as is sometimes supposed, but rather the day of judgment. (The six verses that follow substantiate that fact.) So every time a Christian chooses to obey God by assembling with the saints, he also engages in the vital function of edification; he encourages fellow Christians in their commitment to live for Jesus.

While every aspect of worship is to strengthen the worshiper's relationship with God, it also serves to edify others. For example, the individual Christian's singing is for the purpose of praising God, but it is also for "teaching and admonishing one another" (Colossians 3:16). God designed worship for us to build up one another—to edify the church.

Edification through Preaching

Preachers are to edify the body of Christ (Ephesians 4:11–12). To receive edification from the pulpit, Christians must be present for the preaching, listen attentively, and apply the message. For some in the audience, applying the message results in repentance—resolving to do what they have neglected and resolving to abstain from overt sins. For others it means being encouraged and reassured in the pursuit of God's will. Yet God knew

Christians needed to be reminded often of the temporary nature of this life and the eternal nature of the next. He chose to present that message through preaching. Paul encouraged a young preacher not to "give heed to fables and endless genealogies, which minister questions, rather than godly edifying which is in faith: so do" (1 Timothy 1:4 KJV). What timeless advice for preachers: Stay away from falsities and stay with the faith! When biblical teachings from a Bible-based pulpit fall on the hearts of faithful hearers, the local church is edified.

Edification through Christian Association

Paul teaches that Christians must avoid evil associations (1 Corinthians 15:33). Why did an inspired apostle teach that? Because God wished to warn Christians that the people and events of daily life impact our thinking and, ultimately, our future—even our eternal future! That is why edification through Christian association is so important to building up the local church. One brother, now a deacon, said that upon his conversion he had to give up his old friends, along with his old habits. His choice was difficult, and in the minds of some, extreme. But it came as a result of his calculating the cost (Luke 14:28). Worldly friends have worldly values. When a person determines to live for Christ, he must sacrifice worldly values, including worldly friends who unduly influence him.

When a Christian's primary associates are Christians, his godliness and the godliness of those with whom he associates will increase. The Bible says to Christians: "Therefore encourage one another and build up one another" (1 Thessalonians 5:11). Who understands the intimate struggles and temptations of living for Christ better than saints do? Christ-like relations among Christian families benefit the entire congregation (Ephesians

4:16). The best way to begin to build up the faith of fellow-Christians is to get to know them. Is there any room in a congregation for Christian strangers? Absolutely not! Building up our spiritual family is the most important building project of all. The method of such edification is clearly drawn up in the divine blueprints. Christians interested in edifying their brothers and sisters are careful with the words they choose, actions in which they engage, and interests they pursue. Before engaging in an activity, they ask, "How will this impact the church? How will it affect my brothers and sisters? If it harms them or their spirituality, I will never do it." Such an attitude builds up the local church!

THE BOND THAT BINDS

Heartily singing "I love thy kingdom,"
To God we give our solemn word.
We tell Him we've given His children the sum
Of our care, fraternal love all assured.

We zealously try to love one another;
Our heart is for our brother's welfare.
Since the church was bought by our elder Brother,
We try all her burdens to bear.

'Tis easy to love when harmony prevails;
'Tis tougher when we closer become.
Whichever the case, true love never fails;
It bears gently and helps overcome.

Unlovable, true, some brethren may be;
In error some tend to divide.
If a rebuke or a comfort, let everyone see
The motive of love at our side.

With heaven for a home and earth a brief stay,
We press on with God's family, hearts above.
Encouraging the good and forbearing those astray,
Walk as one under Christ's banner of love!

MAKING IT PRACTICAL

- *Entertain all members of the local congregation in your home.* Before you say "wow, that's impossible," try dividing and conquering. Using the church directory, alphabetically develop several groups of similar size and invite one group at a time. So what if it takes three months—or a year! Your hospitality will pay big dividends—first to you, as you become better acquainted with God's people, and then to your brothers and sisters who will experience new and renewed fellowship.

  Here is a Sunday night plan that will work.

  1. Serve snacks or a simple meal. Have guests provide finger foods or, if you decide to provide a simple meal, have others bring side dishes while you provide the main dish. Paper plates make for faster clean up and give more time for the main reason you're entertaining.
  2. Assign someone to bring songbooks. Not only does singing unite groups, but it provides a means of worship in an informal environment.
  3. Accept without question when someone declines your invitation. You cannot know personal situations. Because of your graciousness, you might later have an opportunity to encourage the downtrodden and weary.

- *Develop and maintain an active visitation program.* A good visitation program promotes good relationships and involves the entire church in a good work. Keep fresh ideas flowing so the program will not become stale.

  1. Realize there are peripheral members who might never be a real part of the Lord's work

without faithful members who show love and provide guidance.

2. Look beyond discouraging events to fruitful ones. Nobody said a visitation program is easy to maintain. Some of those you try to visit will not be at home—or will not appear to be at home. Others will demonstrate their lack of appreciation by making countless promises— unfulfilled promises. Continue your work and you will eventually hear these words: "Thank you for coming by. I do have a problem that I am not spiritual enough to handle. In my weakness, I have almost given up."

3. Remember your coworkers. They are human, too, and they need spiritual exercise. Your faithfulness in a visitation program edifies the faithful.

• *Encourage the elders to maintain contact with all the members.* God never intended shepherds to be CEOs ruling from an office. They must be among the flock. Other members who care can provide much encouragement to spiritual overseers by being active in visitation.

1. Elders set the tone for the congregation in all areas of its work.

2. Elders are selected according to their qualifications, one of which is "given to hospitality" (1 Timothy 3:2 KJV; Titus 1:8).

3. Forming proper relationships within a congregation begins with the leadership.

• *Help your preacher to be well rounded in his presentations.* Preachers are people too. They like to be liked. Their sweet messages receive more compliments than their hell-fire and brimstone ones, so preachers sometimes gravitate to that which satisfies the audience.

1. Preachers must use the right building material. They must not commit the fatal mistake of divorcing healthy, biblical preaching from proper edification.
2. Preachers must edify the church by rebuking and convicting members of their sin, much as a doctor chastises his patients who refuse to care for their bodies.
3. Preachers must also present truths about God's abundant blessings for the faithful and the mutual love we must have for each other.

- *Spend quality time with difficult brothers and sisters.* Getting close to someone of whom others say, "I just don't need to develop relationships with people like that," is not easy. A regular visitation program is not likely to fulfill the needs of those who don't fit the typical member profile.

1. Accept the task of edifying all members of the congregation. All Christians are part of the body of Christ.
2. Challenge yourself to cross socio-economic barriers and move between cultures.
3. Cultivate mutual interests with those who need you most but are less likely to let you know.

QUESTIONS FOR THOUGHT

1. What situations or matters can keep worship from edifying the worshiper?

2. What subjects or what types of sermons do you find most edifying?

3. Find at least three Bible passages that address in principle or by example how the early church was built up by fellowship.

4. How can friendships with the world disrupt our relationship with God? With other Christians?

5. Why do you think God calls all Christians to show hospitality to one another?

CHAPTER FOUR

Education

Know the Book

All men need what God gave Solomon miraculously: "a wise and discerning heart" (1 Kings 3:12). That kind of heart comes only through fervent and constant Bible study.

Every congregation needs to be filled with people who know "the Book" (Hosea 4:6). In view of the delight of biblical information (Psalm 119:16, 24, 35, 47), every congregation needs to be filled with men, women, and children who intimately know "what saith the Scripture." With respect to the demand for biblical incorruptibility, every congregation needs to be filled with those who "do not turn to the right nor to the left" (Proverbs 4:27). What a great privilege one is afforded through the education program of the church! What an opportunity for the student to learn more about the mind and will of God! What a challenge faces Bible teachers!

God commanded group Bible study in the first century (1 Timothy 4:13). Common sense reveals the value of coming together to reason about what God has to say to men (Isaiah 1:18). Since the Book of books will judge every individual, we who know and obey the law are well served (John 12:48). A congregation that gives close attention and concerted effort to the Bible school will always be a growing and thriving congregation!

Train Teachers to Teach the Bible

How important is the Bible teacher? H. G. Adams said, "A teacher affects eternity; he can never tell where his influence stops." The minds of both big and little people are shaped by the instruction they receive. We need to make a continued effort to train teachers to teach the Bible effectively.

The most desirable quality for a Bible teacher is knowledge of the Bible; it can't be beat!

> Insight into human action
> Surely is a treasure,
> But knowledge of the Holy Book
> Rewards beyond all measure.
> Understanding of an earthly matter
> Makes earthly living sweet,
> But understanding what God says
> Never can be beat!
> —Unknown

Attitude and Environment

The successful impartation of God's will for man requires a teacher who has a personal knowledge of God's will (2 Timothy 2:15; 1 Peter 3:15). And the teacher must have a proper attitude. If he is enthusiastic about teaching, his students will likely be enthusiastic about learning. If he demonstrates a love of God's Word, he is more likely to instill it in his students. Few things pour water on the candle of learning more than a lethargic, unprepared, unconcerned, or intimidating teacher. Only the ringing of the bell to end the class will awaken or delight his students!

There is also the need to control the classroom environment. Potential unruliness lurks in any classroom, especially in those of younger children. Inquisitive students are not problems, but indifferent students can be.

Determined students are not problems, but disruptive students are. Class participators are not problems, but class clowns are. Like other areas of effective teaching, class control is a joint effort between teacher and student and, with children, teachers and parents.

We Need Homework

Students should review their previous lesson and make preparation for the next one. When students begin to apply what they learn, the teaching will suddenly become more effective. Homework assignments are effective tools for involving students, but each teacher should decide how best to plant the seed in the heart of the student. Yet, plant he must (1 Corinthians 2:13; 2 Timothy 2:24).

We Need a Good Curriculum

- *Sound in doctrine* (Titus 2:1). If the material teaches false doctrine, it damages the mind and jeopardizes the soul.

- *Age appropriate* (1 Peter 2:2; Hebrews 6:1–2). Consider both the chronological and spiritual ages of those in the audience. New Christians must be fed a different diet from those who are more grounded and settled in truth.

- *Logical in progression.* Jumping erratically from subject to subject or from book to book confuses the students. Logical progression prevents repeating some lessons while skipping others. A systematic approach to Bible study provides the student a more comprehensive understanding of Scripture.

The Cold Harbor Road congregation developed a curriculum that covers the Old Testament in three years and the New Testament in two. Ideally, the five-year cycle will take every child—beginning at age two—through the Bible three times before his or her high school graduation. That congregation is driven by a keen desire to give their children the highest possible quality education in the Bible. Many congregations recognize the need to implement thorough, comprehensive programs of study to equip their students of all ages.

We Need Faithful Attendance

Everyone, from babies to adults, should be enrolled in a Bible class. Bible classes are assemblies of the saints, and they should not be forsaken (Hebrews 10:25). Classes provide opportunities for learning; we should seize these opportunities (Proverbs 1:5). Classes provide moments of meditation; they should be cherished (1 Timothy 4:15). What else could one want to do with his time when the church is assembled for the purpose of studying God's word? (Psalm 122:1).

Attendance that edifies includes being present on time. Arriving late not only disrupts the class, but it also prevents us from fully benefiting from the class. Emergencies occasionally arise, but it is inexcusable to make a habit of straggling in well after the appointed time. Tardiness is inconsiderate. It leaves the impression that our study of God's Word is not a high priority. Effective Bible classes require full participation for the entire class period. That is impossible for those who arrive late.

Behind the growing congregation is the well-constructed Bible school program. Behind the well-constructed Bible school program are the tireless efforts of dedicated Christians. Inside the dedicated Christians beat hearts of love and desire for pleasing God and sharing His will with as many souls as possible. And churches built by people like that will grow!

When You Are Gone

An empty pew, when left by you,
Is such a sad revelation.
For no matter why, it says that my
Family is touched by tribulation.

Physical sickness, pain, or weakness
May place you in dire condition.
Bedfast and worn, by illness torn,
You need prayers and loving attention

And you wish to be back with the church family.
Though circumstances might cause prohibition,
I pray that that wall may eventually fall,
And you will be back "in commission."

But oh if your chair is continually bare,
And bad health is not your attrition,
If in what you partake causes you to forsake
Then you're absent by conscious volition.

Why not come back today, go no longer astray,
In view of both heaven and perdition,
Faithful means you're a part, in both body and heart,
Make amends and improve your situation.

Making It Practical

- *Teachers' skills:* Set as a goal at least one organized activity annually that will improve your teachers' classroom skills. This activity may be a teachers' training session; watching a video series on teaching; or attending a program that teaches mechanics, resource gathering, and methods of teaching. Whatever money and effort this requires of the congregation will pay off in an improved Bible school program.

- *Teachers' awards:* Have a banquet in their honor, in which you give them a token of appreciation and a certificate of recognition. Have the elders publicly commend them. Have sermons preached on the blessing of good Bible teachers.

- *Students' awards:* Give special recognition to students with perfect attendance records and students who bring friends. Challenge students to memorize the books of the Bible or a certain number of Bible verses. Give Bibles to those who meet the challenge. Praise them in the classroom and before their parents. We all thrive on praise, don't we?

- *Coordinators' enlistment:* Appoint individuals to serve as coordinators or department heads of the Bible school program. The greater number of competent individuals who can be enlisted to meet teacher, student, and supply needs, the more positive attention the program will receive. Have an active, qualified deacon to oversee this special program.

- *Special workdays:* Plan periodic workdays to spruce up the learning environment. Bulletin boards should be changed regularly. Pictures of students or church activities and members often draw students' attention. Create a warm environment by choosing favorable paint colors for the wall and colorful, attractive wall décor. Have the room adequately supplied with maps, projectors, and overhead lighting.

- *Resource room:* Have a resource room adequately stocked with teaching supplies. Purchase filing cabinets to correspond with lesson plans or your curriculum, and then fill them with handwork and other auxiliary materials. Have materials for children of all ages. Make it a challenge to continually find new resources with attractive, high quality material. This project will involve many members, which serves at least two purposes. The Solomon principle, "Two are better than one" (Ecclesiastes 4:9), is appropriate here. Competent volunteers working together can accomplish so much more than one person trying to do it all. The other purpose served is that by increasing the involvement and commitment of those members, you increase the likelihood that they will remain faithful to the Lord and His church.

- *Special events:* Education takes in ever-important events such as gospel meetings, seminars, workshops, and lectureships. Churches that adequately plan for and follow up on such activities help to boost the educational program of the local church. We should never miss an opportunity to feed on the bread of life.

QUESTIONS FOR THOUGHT

1. What three qualities of a church education program do you believe to be most essential? What qualities do you think are overrated or given too much emphasis? Explain.

2. Do you believe we have ceased to be the "people of the Book"? If so, what do we need to do to overcome our deficiency?

3. What are some qualities that make a most efficient, effective curriculum? How important is it for classes to be coordinated with each other?

4. What are some "habits" of teachers that discourage an effective education program? What qualities did your favorite childhood teachers exhibit that helped you learn the Bible?

5. What are some ways parents can be involved in the education program of the church?

6. At what age or grade level do you think the plan of salvation should be assertively taught as part of the curriculum?

CHAPTER FIVE

Elimination

Constant Vigilance

There is truth to the saying, "Sometimes you grow through subtraction." That statement has been made in regard to the needful though painful activity of church discipline. Withdrawing fellowship from the disorderly Christian serves as a warning to those living in rebellion to God's holy will. It also expresses love for the soul of the one disfellowshipped. Church discipline has divine purpose. When done correctly—in the proper spirit and with great patience—the church will grow in strength, if not in number.

Additionally, the local church will always grow when each member gets rid of the sin "which so easily entangles" him or her (Hebrews 12:1). Culling out and cleaning up what is personally amiss are two works that demand our constant vigilance (1 Peter 5:8). What should be eliminated from the local congregation? Immorality and worldliness, jealous envy, doctrinal impurity, and trivial bickering—these traits need to be extinct in the church. A close scrutiny of each characteristic proves the necessity of getting rid of them.

Immorality and Worldliness

The Bible repeatedly admonishes God's people to rid themselves of evil. Paul instructed the Ephesian Christians to put off the corrupt and lustful "old self" (Ephe-

sians 4:22) and the multiplied evil deeds of the uncon-
verted "old self" (Colossians 3:8–9). He further commanded them to put out of the mind and body the deeds
of darkness (Romans 13:12) and lay aside the conduct
which displeases God (1 Peter 2:1). One who professes to
imitate Christ will not be spiritually characterized by
words like *darkness, corrupt,* and *wicked* (1 Peter 2:21;
1 Corinthians 11:1). The Christian who loves worldly
things and worldly ways does not have God's approval
(1 John 2:15–17). Making friends with the world is a sure
sign that one is God's enemy (James 4:4). Nothing stops
church growth faster than a worldly, ungodly Christian.

Jealous Envy

Good works are thwarted, good names are slandered,
and good relationships are strained in a church where
envy lives. The word *envy* occurs ten times in the New
Testament. Here is what the Bible says about envy's destructive nature.

- Envy sent Christ to the cross (Matthew 27:18; Mark
  15:10).

- Envy sent Joseph to a foreign land (Acts 7:9).

- Envy sent Paul and Barnabas from the Jews to the
  Gentiles (Acts 13:45).

- Envy sent Thessalonica into a chaotic uproar (Acts
  17:5).

- Envy sent the Gentiles into the way of spiritual
  depravity and death (Romans 1:29).

- Envy sent some preachers into a hypocritical state
  (Philippians 1:15).

- Envy puts false teachers in a position to split
  churches (1 Timothy 6:4).

- Envy puts a person in bad company (Titus 3:3).

- Envy puts one on the wrong side of God (James 4:5).

How angry it must make God when one song leader becomes jealous of another! How disturbing it must be to Him to see a couple jealous because a couple friendly to them spends time with other families. How silly, but destructive, when jealousy rears its ugly head in the congregation (Romans 13:13; 1 Corinthians 3:3; Galatians 5:26; James 3:14, 16). God will call into account such foolishness.

Doctrinal Impurity
Despite what we hear to the contrary, God teaches that doctrine matters! The doctrine must be

- Distinct (1 Timothy 1:3)
- Sound (healthy, uncorrupt) (1 Timothy 1:10)
- Good (1 Timothy 4:6)
- Godly (1 Timothy 6:3)
- Of Christ (Hebrews 6:1).

Whatever is not the doctrine of Christ is false and rejected by God (2 John 9–10). Though many are turning from the cross to chase the carnally minded and to appease the spiritually ill, the church must overcome the temptation to water down or apologize for the truth of the gospel (Romans 1:16). Compromising and changing the Bible must never be. But if it ever does infect the church, it must be eliminated.

In one of the cruelest, most tragic practical jokes ever played, three Florida teenagers removed a stop sign from a busy intersection. Consequently, three other young people lost their lives in a multi-car crash. The pranksters were given stiff prison sentences, but those lost lives cannot be retrieved. How sickening that they could find humor in doing something so morbidly sinister!

Yet, long ago Solomon said, "Do not move the ancient boundary which your fathers have set" (Proverbs 22:28). It is dangerous for anyone to remove the stop signs that God has erected in His Word. The only way to do all in the name of the Lord is to remove the unauthorized green lights and observe the stop signs God put up along the way (John 14:6), that is, teach what Christ has taught and stand where He stands!

Trivial Bickering

Too often the church condescends into squabbles over the ridiculously insignificant. These private battles have been known to divide the church. When a congregation divides over carpet colors, head coverings, time of services, and other matters of judgment, that church has been mortally wounded. Its influence is slaughtered. Its effectiveness is amputated. Its soul-winning capabilities are handicapped. Debates with false teachers are declining, and properly, kindly conducted ones need a revival among God's people. But debating within the church over the inconsequential is sinful (1 Corinthians 3:3; Philippians 2:3; James 3:14–16). To preserve the unity among the saints, such bickering and wrangling must be eliminated. Like shedding those extra pounds, the excess dead weight of sin must be dropped to promote the growth of the Lord's church.

Samuel Feldman is the world's most famous bread vandal. He did eight thousand dollars worth of damage to bread and cookies throughout the Yardley, Pennsylvania, area a few years ago. He was going around squeezing, smashing, and poking bags of bread and packages of cookies. Finally, one store, suspecting Feldman, put him under surveillance and caught him three times in the act. He was charged with one count of criminal mischief. An idle person with a mean spirit caused three years of aggravation and loss.

There is usually at least one "bread-squeezer" in every group, including the local church. These are the nitpickers, storm clouds who live to rain on others' parades—those who seem to enjoy causing friction and irritating others, those who hold petty grudges, and general pot-stirrers. Each of us should follow the example of the disciples in asking, "Surely not I, Lord?" (Matthew 26:22). The church is always in need of more encouraging, uplifting, positive, happy, and contented members. These, not the bread-squeezers, build up the local church.

THE TURNAROUND

Face toward sin, though scorching hot,
I tread to reach its surging bounty.
Then, tasting it, bitter sorrow and not
At all a pleasant journey.
I contemplated, then took again
From Satan's wilting tree—
The bitter, poisonous fruit of sin.
Now, vexed, I wanted to flee.
When gospel truth my conscience tore;
Gave me hope that I could be whole,
I strove to leave the lusts which war
Against my precious soul.
Now face toward God and back toward sin,
I humbly walk before the Light.
Though tattered without, now whole within,
I resist the foe with all God's might!

MAKING IT PRACTICAL

Unpopular Preaching

There are several subjects, though quite unpopular, that must be addressed with some regularity because of the immoral world in which we live. These lessons, once commonplace, are now rarely heard. Preachers may either fear a loss of popularity or job security, or they may not be convinced of the sinfulness of these matters. Elders or other prominent church leaders may fear the negative effect such "restrictive" sermons or Bible class lessons would have on contented church members. Yet the need is greater than ever for sermons on worldliness.

- Immodesty, among other things, involves the wearing of apparel that accentuates or reveals the body in a way that produces a normal response of lust in the heart of another.

- Dancing involves many of the same problems as does immodesty, but it further provides opportunity for body contact.

- Social drinking not only supports an exceedingly sinful industry, but it also impairs the mind and influence of any who engage in it.

- Immoral entertainment—movies, music, TV shows, and Web sites that portray nudity, sexuality, violence, and bad language—are inappropriate for Christian consumption.

- "And such like." Similar activities that lead to sin, that harm the body or mind, or cause one to become a stumbling block must be avoided. Christians infected with any worldliness lead others away from Christ.

Exemplary Role Models

Preachers and teachers at our learning institutions have a wonderful opportunity to model charity and magnanimous behavior. Men in such positions have a great responsibility to avoid preacher envy, becoming adversarial with those seen as rivals—not to mention seeing brethren as rivals in the first place—and becoming drunk with power, whether real or perceived. How many brotherhood squabbles have had such pettiness as their motives? These things impact local churches, which often line up behind "their man" or "their school."

Parents, elders, and concerned Christians should help young people find a Christian university or training school that will encourage and reinforce the moral lessons they grew up learning in their homes and congregation. Go the extra mile to learn the school's view of the Bible's inspiration and its application. Young people who go away to schools will probably become leaders in local churches. Let us help steer them toward influences that build their morality as well as their morale.

Stop the Gossip

This often-told story bears repeating. A preacher kept a black book which he pulled out when a "concerned" church member came by to express his angst over the behavior of another or to pass along some "news" he had heard about a brother or sister. Before complaining member could begin, the preacher opened the black book with pen in hand and said, "Wait. I want to write it down exactly as you say it. Then I would like you to sign your name to it." Throughout his preaching career, he never made a single entry in his black book. Gossip is a sin (2 Corinthians 12:20).

Gauge for Doing Right

How can you determine whether a thought, an act, a recreation, a practice, a lifestyle, or a habit is right or wrong? Carefully consider the following questions.

- Do you want to be engaged in this activity at the moment of Christ's return?

- Can you defend the thought or deed before Christ at the judgment?

- Do you want your mate, parents, children, preacher, elders, or other Christians you respect to see you practice this activity?

- Do you want it in your possession—in your thoughts, on your tongue, in your pockets, or in your cabinets—when the record of your life is opened before all?

- If Christ were sitting nearby watching you, would you do or say the thing?

- Is there concern that engaging in the activity will cost you your soul?

- Does it prevent you from drawing closer to God?

- Does it harm your influence for Christ? What if a person knows you are a Christian and discovers your action?

- Do you really think Christ would do it?

Questions for Thought

1. How common is envy among God's people? What causes it? How does it show itself?

2. Why do elderships hesitate to deal with false teaching from the pulpit and classroom?

3. List some proactive methods congregations can use to ground members doctrinally. If you have seen these methods at work, tell why they are effective.

4. Discuss some common causes of bickering and personality conflicts within a congregation. What is the most effective way to cope with these issues?

5. How does Christian education cause or hinder church growth?

CHAPTER SIX

Enthusiasm

With All Your Might

As one's physical body will die without its heart, so will the local body of Christ that fails to care about the lost, the Lord's will, and the brethren. Indifference will kill a congregation. Surely the Lord saw in Simon the Zealot (Luke 6:15) a key element that, under His influence, would help "turn the world upside down" (Acts 17:6 KJV) and cause him to be "zealous for good deeds" (Titus 2:14). The Lord wants all His people to have great zeal, based on sufficient knowledge of His Word (Romans 10:2).

One of the words translated "zeal" in the New Testament describes an emotion that can either be good or evil. When it describes jealous indignation (Acts 5:17), envy (Acts 13:45 KJV; Romans 13:13 KJV), or emulations (Galatians 5:20 KJV), it is shown to be evil and condemning. The idea is of a passionate emotion that causes one to work earnestly toward the accomplishment of whatever goal is in mind. The Lord has given Christians noble goals with eternal implications. Soul winning spells the difference in where neighbors, friends, and co-workers will dwell in the never-ending eternity. Uplifting fellow Christians through encouragement or rebuke influences the same difference in their eternal goal to be in heaven. The exhortation from the wisdom literature rings out for us today as much as it ever should have for the Israelites. In Ecclesiastes 9:10 the reader is admonished:

"Whatever your hand finds to do, do it with all your might"!

With the thunder of heaven's authority, Paul cried, "For this reason it says, 'Awake, sleeper, and arise from the dead, and Christ will shine on you'" (Ephesians 5:14). As it was in Isaiah's day, M. W. Spencer writes that even in our time "there is much to do, there's work on every hand" (Isaiah 6:8). But who cares? Christians must care! They must demonstrate that concern by asking the leadership, "What of the much work that is on every hand can I do?"

Enthusiasm Is Everybody's Business

Can everyone visit? Can everyone write notes of encouragement? Can everyone be involved in the generation, production, and teaching of the Bible school? Can everyone attend Bible class to build personal faith? Can everyone invite others to attend the assemblies? The answer is yes, unless in some extreme circumstance one is physically unable. Then God knows and understands.

Christian Worker Bees

A natural crisis is developing across our nation—the honey worker bees are disappearing, and nobody knows exactly why. The most disturbing aspect is there are no dead bodies anywhere and the hives look normal on the outside. Theories include pesticides, predators, and people (of course), but nothing is apparent. Bees pollinate one-third of the world's food supply, but whoever gives thought to these quiet, diligent workers?

Think about how many in the church are like the honey bee. They work almost undetectably, unheralded behind the scenes. Without them much work would go undone. Occasionally, these workers may get discouraged by lack of appreciation, opposition, or criticism. They might give up and "disappear." Yet, think about congregations without these quiet workers. Bulletin boards aren't decorated. Kitchens aren't cleaned. Tract racks aren't stocked. Shut-ins and sick folks aren't contacted. Cards aren't sent. New Christians and new members aren't exhorted. Visits aren't made. Individually, these workers may not be able to do much, but collectively their impact is huge! Their works may be most noticeable when they are not around to do them anymore. Those who work like these honey bees deserve honor and recognition. Their work is significant and essential.

Enthusiasm Is a Natural Spiritual Response

Two words are vital in this discussion. Of course, with reference to Christians, the word *everyone* is important. No one is exempt from obeying God, but also consider the word *enthusiastic*. Never should Christian deeds and obedience be rote, matter-of-fact, and heartless. With enthusiasm, the Christian must eagerly work at the tasks given by Christ. As he told the Laodiceans, Christ tells every Christian today to "be zealous" (Revelation 3:19). What if there were more Epaphrases in the local church? (Colossians 4:12–13). Epaphras agonized intensely over his brethren as he prayed for them (v. 12). He not only prayed for them but did so with great fervor. Further, he had an overflowing desire for his brethren (v. 13). His heart was with God's people! In practical terms, what will one do for his brethren for whom he has such feelings?

When a brother is in error, will a caring Christian not seek for him? (James 5:19–20). When a brother is lonely or discouraged, will a caring Christian not lift him? (Hebrews 12:12–13). When a brother stands for the truth, even when his stand draws the world's criticism, will a caring Christian not praise him? (1 Corinthians 11:2). Finally, Epaphras was a loyal servant of his brethren in Christ (Colossians 1:7). Undoubtedly, he loved fellow Christians and made himself available to them.

Enthusiasm Must Be Trained

Many are passionate about the wrong things. They have invested in something with a terrible eternal yield. In 1995, outside the Bulgarian Embassy in Washington, D.C., the son of a former embassy employee lost his life. Walking with his friends, he was confronted by muggers. Apparently, however, his murder could have been averted! The thieves only wanted his jacket. He resisted and fought until one of the agitated criminals killed him. Now, without benefit of an opened police report our imaginations soar. What was so special about that jacket? What made the coat worth a human life to its young possessor— its age, design, or material? Why didn't he just give up that jacket? It simply meant too much to him.

Our passions are always with us, so we must train them. Our greatest interest must be in spiritual things. Our time, money, and energy should be adequately poured into areas that reflect our spiritual interest. Lot's wife gave up her life for a single glance back at Sodom (Genesis 19:26). Korah gave up his life for a run at power (Numbers 16:31–35). Achan gave up his life for, among other trifling things, some Babylonish garments and a bit of wealth (Joshua 7:21–25 KJV). Samson gave up his life for relief from the nagging of a wicked, heathen woman (Judges 16:17–30). Absalom gave up his life for a seat on a throne (2 Samuel 18:14–15). Ahab gave up his life for a vineyard (1 Kings 22:29–38). Haman gave up his life for a bow from Mordecai (Esther 3:2; 7:9–10). Judas gave up his life for twenty-five dollars (Zechariah 11:12). Ananias and Sapphira gave up their lives for an infinitesimal percentage of the world's riches (Acts 5:1–10). Some early Christians gave up their lives for brief pleasure (1 Timothy 5:6).

Christians must give up their lives. We must give ourselves to the Lord (2 Corinthians 8:5). We must lose our lives for His sake (Luke 17:33). We must sacrifice ourselves on the altar of service (Romans 12:1–2). If we will spend ourselves in service to God, it will capture our affections. We may begin serving out of duty, but that service will grow into something wonderfully joyous (Acts 20:24; Hebrews 13:17).

As with the church of Christ in Corinth (2 Corinthians 7:10–11), there is a need for every congregation of God's people to repent of sins and then to revive its spirit and work at its tasks with enthusiasm! When non-Christian visitors and others are among a righteous, zealous congregation, they will want to know why all the fuss. Then they too will want to be among those who have "devoted themselves to the ministry of the saints" (1 Corinthians 16:15).

A "TELL" OF TWO CHURCHES

We worshiped with a congregation,
A church in God's own fold.
Song and sermon brought elation,
But afterward the saints were cold.

In the aisle we braced to shake
As the church all hastened by.
Not an elder, deacon, member spake;
The preacher weakly told us "hi."

We stood around the foyer
A couple of moments more,
But no one greeted us that Lord's day
So we sadly left and closed the door.

We worshiped with another group,
A church sound in "the way."
Their singing grand, the preaching true,
But after came the test that day.

A sister grabbed us by the arm!
She said, "Come over for lunch."
Six deacons asked, "Where are you from?"
Smiles and shakes came by the bunch!

The preachers and elders chatted awhile;
We felt among close kin!
We left that day, each with a smile.
Friend, which church would you fit in?

MAKING IT PRACTICAL

- *Invest in God's work.* Enthusiasm is directly connected to involvement. The greater our involvement in the work that the church is doing, the more invested our feelings become. It is wrong to suggest that one always feels enthusiastic about church work, whether in the beginning of the work or in the middle of it. One may have second thoughts about becoming more involved in a church program. It may lose its initial luster or excitement. Yet enthusiasm speaks to a sustained, genuine interest in things spiritual.

- *Use your talents.* Find areas of church life that best fit your interests and best use your talents. However, gauge how weighted your interest is in areas of work that may seem more glamorous or fun compared with those requiring a bigger heart of service. There are never too many Christians filling the role of servants in the kingdom.

- *Have an attitude of adventure.* If an activity requires you to insert your own enthusiasm, such as door-knocking, cleaning the baptistry, visiting someone confined to home, cleaning the building, or preparing the communion, find ways to make those activities more enjoyable. Ask a Christian friend to join you. Look at the activity as an adventure or learning experience. Pray about your attitude.

- *Watch your face.* Give conscious attention to "little things" such as facial expressions, tone of voice, and other nonverbal cues that may suggest you are less than enthusiastic about doing church work. Enthusiasm begets enthusiasm.

- *Show care and concern.* The January 7, 2001, edition of a Birmingham, Alabama, newspaper carried the story about a worker who was dead at his desk for five days before anyone noticed. The 51-year-old man had been employed as a proofreader at a New York firm for thirty years. He had a heart attack in the office he shared with twenty-three other workers. He quietly passed away on Monday, but none of his coworkers noticed. On Saturday morning a weekend worker came through the office and asked why he was working on the weekend.

- We must have care and concern, byproducts of spiritual zeal, to be keenly aware of the spiritual condition of our co-workers in Christ. Let a zeal for the Lord's house, the church, consume us (John 2:17).

- *Do these three things.* Art Linkletter's remarks, when 84 years old, about his ability to stay vibrant, happy, and successful are often repeated: "You need three things—something to do, something to love, and something to hope for." Applied to Christian living, we have all three in the local church.

There is more work to do than the local church can ever fully accomplish. We have one another, the lost, and the Lord to love. We have heaven as our abiding hope. If these will not create enthusiasm within us, we have a serious heart problem that needs healing.

QUESTIONS FOR THOUGHT

1. Enthusiasm is a natural byproduct of Christianity. Why? List some things that dampen congregational enthusiasm.

2. How do Christians motivate themselves to be enthusiastic about less glamorous tasks: work days, visiting the downtrodden, pleading with an erring Christian to return to the Lord?

3. A warm smile and an effervescent personality are marks of enthusiasm. How else is enthusiasm for spiritual things demonstrated?

4. How can you help to create enthusiasm in another member?

5. Name some programs that build congregational enthusiasm.

CHAPTER SEVEN

Eldership

In his *Christian Leadership Handbook,* J. J. Turner lists twelve reasons that he believes the church has seen a decline in quality, scriptural leadership:

- The tendency to take the path of least resistance.
- Falling into a routine that has become "hum-drum."
- A lack of training for the job assignment.
- Leaders having too many responsibilities.
- Loss of interest in the work assigned or position accepted.
- Personality problems among leaders.
- A communication gap between leaders and followers.
- Failure to add "new blood" to existing leadership.
- Lack of appreciation.
- The entrance of sin into the leadership ranks.
- Discouragement.
- Thinking the challenge has been met.

Liberalism and radicalism, when they infiltrate congregations, often come through sinful actions or inactions of the leadership. Who is responsible when a preacher is allowed to preach divisive or false doctrine? Who is accountable for dealing with those who walk disorderly? Who will answer if the flock gets improper spiritual food, goes astray, or is devoured by wolves from within?

Elders Are Part of a Divine Plan

Anyone who has sat in a men's business meeting can appreciate this truth. Anyone who has not sat in a men's business meeting deserves to do so at least once in order to appreciate God's plan. Of course, some congregations do not yet have two men qualified to serve as elders. Such churches must have an alternate means of making decisions. Yet, the idea is to do everything possible to work toward having elders in every congregation (Titus 1:5).

The eldership is one of the primary indicators that determines congregational growth. Having elders to oversee the congregation is God's wisdom. He designed His church (Ephesians 3:11) to function with a plurality of elders (1 Timothy 3:1–7; Titus 1:5–9). A plurality of qualified men with diverse personalities leading the church in walking in God's truth is, by His deliberate design, God's superior plan. When the right men lead the right way, the flock is fed (Acts 20:28), the disorderly are marked and disciplined (Romans 16:17 KJV; 2 Thessalonians 3:6–15), the activity within the congregation is known by these overseers (1 Peter 5:2), and the congregation has in its elders phenomenal examples of true Christianity.

Elders Are Leaders Who Must Be Followed

In order for the congregation with good, sound leaders to grow, she must respond properly to those leaders. The elders have authority over the congregation (Hebrews 13:7). The church is to be obedient and submissive to her elders (Hebrews 13:17). If her leaders do not depart from the doctrine of Christ, the church must follow their leadership. Accusations levied against an elder must not be easily accepted or believed (1 Timothy 5:19). All of these scriptural admonitions teach that elders are to be respected and followed as they walk in the path mapped out by Christ (Matthew 7:13–14).

Elders Influence the Future of the Local Church

The idea that elders may have the single, greatest earthly influence on the direction a church takes must drive godly shepherds to their knees in constant prayer. From where will the church's vision come, planning the works outlined by the Bible? Who will take the lead in promoting the gospel, defending it, and sharing it with the lost? What men will magnify the spirit of Christ so necessary to spiritual and numerical growth? As in so many areas of life, church growth begins at the top. Christ wants growth, and the leaders of His church must work toward the goal while holding firmly to the doctrine of the one who died for the church (Ephesians 5:25) and who will judge her (1 Peter 4:17).

DEAR FATHER, FOR OUR ELDERS

Holy Father, Watcher, Giver,
Overlooking all our hearts,
Proper thanks we'll offer never
For Thy plan for our souls' care.
Thou hast spoken through Thy Word
Wanting Thy flock free from snare,
Commanding men to wisely shepherd.
Thy great stewards from our midst
Are men with feet of clay, and yet
They faithfully follow as Thou bidst
Through each sorrow, care, and fret.
Sacrificial, loving pastors
Careful of the food we're fed,
Fighting sin, submitting to their Master's
Written Word. They love the church's Head.
Could we pay them, Father, truly
What they're worth to body, spirit?

Faithfully they lead us fully,
Hold forth Thy Word, and keep us near it!
As we close, we vow before Thee
That we'll support these godly men
Until we cross death's final sea.
Please bless our elders. In Christ, Amen.

MAKING IT PRACTICAL

Consider the following thoughts about who an elder should be:

- A *spiritual* man whose heart, concern, and life centers around the cross.

- A *genuine* man who loves people unpretentiousnessly and steers clear of church politics.

- A *compassionate* man who is able to shed tears and show emotion over important things.

- An *imperfect* man who, though spiritually mature, knows he is human and understands that I, too, am human and sometimes weak.

- An *approachable* man who garners respect, not through gruffness and intimidation but through warmth and hospitality.

- A *sound* man who demonstrates the ability to discern between truth and error and whose love for God will cause him to vigorously defend His church and doctrine without partiality.

- A *loving* man who demonstrates love at every level—spousal, family, community, church, and God.

- An *active* man who participates with his sleeves rolled up, whose every effort is for Christ and His church.

- A *sensible* man who deliberates, weighs, considers, and decides upon matters with both wisdom and maturity.

- A *qualified* man who meets those qualifications Paul gave through Timothy and Titus, though we know none will ever meet those to perfection.

Wendell Winkler writes in *Leadership: The Crisis of Our Time* about current leadership styles he has observed. He lists eight negative—howbeit often present—leadership styles found in the local church, including the passive, figurehead leader, the reluctant leader, and the micro-manager. Positively, he writes of the servant-leader, shepherd-leader, and participative-leader as the style sorely lacking but so desperately needed today. Every eldership would do well to absorb and apply these principles.

- *Appreciate your elders.* Write them thank-you notes and tell them face-to-face, often, how much you benefit from their leadership and example. Serving as an elder is one of the most thankless, demanding jobs there is. Though they are leaders, they need encouragement like everyone else.

- *Make a commitment to a local congregation.* Consider the matter of "placing membership" or "identifying," as some prefer to call it. When moving into a new area, you will want to make a commitment to a local congregation. While it is foolish to identify with a church without carefully looking into many particulars—none more important than her leadership—at some point a decision is fair and warranted. Some rebuff the idea of placing membership; however, the concept is a biblical one. Elders will give an account for the sheep in the flock where they serve (Hebrews 13:17). How do they know what sheep are under their charge, unless the sheep let them know? By the same token, Christians are to submit to the eldership (Hebrews 13:7, 17). This implies the need to identify. The members of the church as a body, army, and family are accountable to one another (Galatians 6:2; Ephesians 5:21; Romans 12:5). The harvest is as white as ever and the available workers as scant as when Jesus first said as much (John 4:35). Research the works and characteristics of the congregation where you have been visiting, but make the decision to place membership as quickly as you can.

- *Don't forget to encourage the elders' wives.* They are among the most sacrificial, yet most overlooked, women in a congregation. They must endure much and are usually among the church's most active members.

Could You Do Her Job?

"I need your husband, is he there?"
She's heard that o'er and o'er.
Counseling, funerals, weddings, sickness
Take his time and make him walk the floor.

"The elders did or didn't do this,"
Rings differently in her ears.
This is her husband that they speak of;
She holds his hands and sees his tears.

"The elders will boldly take a stand,"
So confidently the Christians cry!
But it is her husband who must take courage,
Rebuke the teaching, look the erring in the eye.

"I need to speak with an elder!"
He's pulled from here and there,
But godly, loving, she supports him;
An elder's wife must really care.

"We really have such good, fine elders";
How wonderful a tribute to report.
But they would never, ever make it
Without wives of prayer and faith and support.

QUESTIONS FOR THOUGHT

1. Someone has said, "The church rises and falls with the leadership." Do you think this is fair? Why or why not?

2. How can the church better prepare young men to serve as shepherds in their later years?

3. How do culture and the home affect a congregation's attitude toward leadership? What can be done to counteract these trends?

4. List some of the most important qualities of leadership? Do you think a compilation of class expectations would challenge the eldership to reach greater heights?

5. Consider this cliché: Preachers do elders' work, elders do deacons' work, and deacons do not know what they should be doing. Does that statement accurately summarize the condition of the leadership in the typical congregational? If your answer is yes, suggest ways to fix the problem?

CHAPTER EIGHT

Effort

A Mind to Work

Von Goethe wrote, "It is not doing the thing which we like to do, but liking to do the thing which we have to do that makes life blessed." Why is it that the lazy find no joy in working, but even the hardest workers tend to derive great pleasure in so doing? A church's success in her mission and goals rely heavily upon people having "a mind to work" (Nehemiah 4:6). In his heartwarming salutation, Paul says to the church of Christ in Thessalonica:

> We give thanks to God always for all of you, making mention of you in our prayers; constantly bearing in mind your work of faith and labor of love and steadfastness of hope in our Lord Jesus Christ in the presence of our God and Father, knowing, brethren beloved by God, His choice of you (1 Thessalonians 1:2–4).

Faith must be accompanied by works (James 2:17). Love is demonstrated by one's labors (John 14:15). Every member of the local church must have a "faith working through love" (Galatians 5:6).

What soul is won without immense effort, often from the collaborative labors of brethren? What successful congregational goal depends on passive Christians? Will the church grow by luck, chance, or mistake? Or rather, will it grow in strength and number through the combined ergonomics of dedicated people of God? The Bible continually stresses the necessity of the local church's involvement in active labor to spread the influence of the gospel and infiltrate the community with the message of hope and peace. Notice the following key thoughts relative to congregational efforts, as emphasized in the Bible.

No Work Is Unimportant

Only glory-seeking individuals rank church works in terms of importance and priority. What purpose is served in exalting one work while ignoring another? What if "my" work is overlooked, but "your" work is honored? Paul reminds Christians: "Therefore, my beloved brethren, be ye stedfast, unmovable, always abounding in the work of the Lord, forasmuch as ye know that your labor is not in vain in the Lord" (1 Corinthians 15:58 KJV).

Any work within the church that needs doing to help achieve the goal of saving souls requires one to make sacrifices. The word *labor* in 1 Corinthians 15:58 means "trouble, pain, and toil." So the work may require giving up time, money, and effort one might have invested elsewhere. Then any work within the church that needs doing to help achieve the goal of saving souls is never futile or unimportant. Paul says no work of the Lord is in vain. Whether janitorial, electrical, mechanical, or spiritual, everyone's labor in the Lord is noted.

Finally, any work that contributes to the salvation of souls must be according to the will of the Lord. Work done "in the Lord" is never without value. That which He permits and directs through His Word to convert or preserve souls is what Christians can do. No one need be idle and without spiritual aim, for there is much to do to strengthen the local church.

Work Ethics Are Important

Some do "church work" to be seen of men (Matthew 6:5; 23:5). Some do "church work" for self-glory (Acts

5:1–11). Some do "church work" for ungodly, ulterior motives (Philippians 1:15–16). *Why* one works is equally as important as *if* one works.

- *Work with the right motive.* Paul says, "Therefore we also have as our ambition, whether at home or absent, to be pleasing to Him" (2 Corinthians 5:9). When volunteering or engaging in a church program, ask, "Am I doing this to be accepted of Christ?"

- *Work with the right goals in mind.* Ask, "What do I hope to gain from my involvement? Is my goal worthy and honorable?" One's goal in doing "church work" may be a sincere desire to help his Christian brethren grow closer to Christ (Colossians 1:28–29). Perhaps one fervently works, keeping his eyes on the reward of heaven (Hebrews 4:11). Let spiritually related objectives spur us on to accomplish church tasks!

- *Work with the right attitude.* Church work can be discouraging. New Christians fall away from active duty. Projects can be frustrating. People can present challenges. Failures come. However, Paul's encouragement to young Timothy spurs on God's people today: "For it is for this we labor and strive, because we have fixed our hope on the living God, who is the Savior of all men, especially of believers" (1 Timothy 4:10). When others are unkind to us, overlook our involvement, or are unaware of what we do for Christ, let us keep cheerfully working by trust in the living God. It matters not what men see us do for Christ but what God sees.

Works Are Noticed

Just as church work undone is painfully obvious, so are good works done for Christ, however quietly. Others see the example of good deeds presented by the Christian worker (Titus 2:7). In the *Sermon on the Mount,* Jesus promised that all people would be known by their fruits (Matthew 7:16–20). Not only will men see good works and thereby glorify the Father (Matthew 5:16), but He also sees and keeps a record of one's works. Hebrews 6:10 says, "For God is not unjust so as to forget your work and the love which you have shown toward His name, in having ministered and in still ministering to the saints." Whether or not the local church remembers our efforts for good is irrelevant; God will not forget. It is as the old song suggests, "Our Lord keeps a record of the moments I'm spending down here" (Revelation 2:2).

Works Are Learned

Titus 3:14 says works are learned through doing. One does not become a worker for the Lord by sitting on the sidelines and watching and admiring the deeds of others. Soul winners, preachers, elders, deacons, teachers, visitors, and others hone their works by doing. Books of theory and strategy are sterile without implementation. The faithfully obedient are doers, not just dreamers (Titus 3:8; Numbers 13:30). They are not fearful of failure, but are scared of slothfulness. They overcome obstacles and conquer cynicism. They learn that good works are habit forming and addictive, just the same as lethargy and uninvolvement. The church that labors is the church in good working order. Though God's people who are following His truth with desire and dedication may occasionally be guilty of making a wrong decision in the realm of judgment or expediency, He understands and can make good come, even of that. He will not excuse a church filled with mere pew sitters and skilled talkers. Before the King, the saved will hear "well done." The unfaithful who talked a good plan but never executed it will not hear "well said."

They will hear far sadder words (Matthew 25:41). Growing churches are filled with active disciples. Servants of God get to work.

Sloths are tropical mammals that live a relatively long life—sometimes more than ten years—almost all of which is spent hanging upside down in trees. They move slowly and deliberately from limb to limb, touching the ground only when necessary. In fact, they seem to dislike the ground so much that, when placed there, they simply lie on their backs and are practically unable to crawl. They sleep during the day; the most noise they make is an occasional whine. They burn as little energy as possible, and are slow in doing that. The terms *slothful* and *sluggard,* obviously borrowed from observers of their habitat, have become synonymous with laziness and indolence (Proverbs 19:24; 26:15–16). God speaks of the slothful as those without initiative (Proverbs 6:6–11), those who are unreliable and irresponsible (Proverbs 10:26), those who had rather wish than work (Proverbs 13:4), and those who want benefit without investment (Proverbs 20:4).

Reliability and usefulness are learned traits, and they are best learned by practice. When church leaders call for workers, we simply cannot sit there idly, confident that "someone" will volunteer. If I am truly a Christian—not just while in the building but everywhere—I will make a commitment and then follow through. Do not over commit but strive to be a Christian others can count on to help the church grow. Many members practice being "busy here and there" (1 Kings 20:40), but remain slothful in response to their Christian duty.

There may be a bit of sluggard in everyone. The tendency to slough off in our duty to the Lord is always a temptation near at hand. The devil surely will use idleness to try to defeat the cause of Christ in the local church.

What wisdom and blessings are found in doing with all our might what our hands find to do! (Ecclesiastes 9:10). Churches that want to grow and will to grow get "to the work"!

A PROVERB TO PONDER

Now, not all our attenders are members,
And not all our members are attenders,
But if all our attenders were members,
And all our members were attenders

THEN . . .
We'd have more trouble menders,
More gospel defenders,
And more true soul winners!

BUT . . .
We'd have fewer people offenders,
Fewer spiritual hinderers,
And fewer religious pretenders!

SO . . .
Let us all render a more tender surrender
To the Commender of a love full of splendor!
As we meander on this earth full of sinners,
Let us engender a life with the Lord at the center.

MAKING IT PRACTICAL

- *Involve recent converts.* Good leadership understands the necessity of involving new Christians in the work of the church as soon as possible, especially those without a background in the church. Good elders and resourceful deacons do so by creating new jobs for new talents.

- *Tap individual potentials.* Church leaders should understand that not everyone has the same personality. It is a mistake to think the potential worker has the same personality we do or that all prospective volunteers can be handled the same way. As far back as Herodotus, it has been recognized that communities are filled with people with at least four broad personality types. Do not pigeonhole people. This makes for a greater challenge in "reading" people and discerning how to approach them, but it pays off in the response of the workers.

- *Continually evaluate the viability and success of the church's programs of work.* Some begin well and then fizzle. Others start slow and then build momentum. Eager participants in good programs sometimes burn out. When this happens, rest the program for a while, reevaluate it, and implement it again. If it continues to lag, try to find other ways to do what the failed program was meant to do.

- *Use talent sheets.* Why let them collect dust in a filing cabinet. These forms are tangible indicators of others' interest in being involved. Deacons who make maximum use of others' talents ease their own loads and help the church accomplish much more than if only a few do the work.

- *Plan and implement "involvement fairs."* They provide opportunities for deacons to share with the local church the works of which they have charge and solicit help. These are usually conducted after a fellowship meal or between the assemblies. Work programs must be presented creatively. At our first "involvement fair," one of our deacons working in evangelism dressed up in battle fatigues sporting the slogan: "We want you." Quirky? Yes, but effective! Thirty-eight members, previously not involved in evangelism, volunteered to help him. The goal is gaining more workers for the harvest (John 4:35).

1. How much does the work ethic of our culture affect the work ethic in the church?

2. What are typical excuses members give for not being involved in the work of the church? Suggest ways to overcome these.

3. What are some needed works the congregation can initiate to enlist workers and better fulfill the purposes the Lord has given to the church? How can the church put these in place?

4. Deacons are often frustrated because they are assigned tasks for which that have not been trained. What steps can be taken to equip them? What cautions are needed? Who do you think should do the training?

5. How can we help youth programs to place more emphasis on service? What can young people do to be involved in the church's work?

CHAPTER NINE

Evangelists

Role of the Preacher

Thom Rainer, in his book *Surprising Insights from the Unchurched: and Proven Ways to Reach Them,* presents some practical methods of winning those with no consistent church backgrounds. (Mr. Rainer is not a member of the church of Christ; he wrote for denominations.) He concluded that the pulpit played a significant role in reaching the unchurched. Indeed, ninety-seven percent of his "353 formerly unchurched" interviewees said the preacher played a part in their decision to adhere. Here are the top five ways the preacher influenced them:

- He taught principles of scripture.
- He made a practical application of those principles to everyday life.
- He was authentic.
- He was passionate in his convictions.
- He demonstrated a personal interest in members of the congregation.

As I read of the preacher's influence on the lives of so many—no doubt representative of a wide cross section of our society—chills ran up and down my spine for several reasons. First, almost all the preachers who mount pulpits in churches around this nation Sunday by Sunday are preaching false doctrine that will lead their congregations to a dismal eternal destination (Matthew 7:13–23). Second, I am a preacher, and God expects more

of those who proclaim His Word than of other members
(James 3:1). Third, people are watching how my walk
matches my talk. Then, it is a long and tiresome process
to lead people away from putting "too much stock" in a
preacher, counteracting a common tendency to elevate
him above what is proper.

The Work of an Evangelist

The preacher, in doing the work of an evangelist, is
not a pastor. The pastors of the church are her elders.
This is one reason it is so important for the elders to
maintain high visibility during the assemblies, in members' homes, at hospitals, at funeral homes, at wedding
chapels, and wherever they can be with the sheep of the
local flock.

Yet the man who finds himself at "center stage" of
the church's life is an important factor in whether or not
the local church will grow and succeed. That is why every preacher of the gospel should make it a weekly habit
to read 1 Timothy, 2 Timothy, and Titus to review the
work of an evangelist. How many times has a great
church been demolished by a preacher of poor quality or
shoddy ethics? How many mediocre churches have been
spurred on to greatness by hardworking, well-trained
evangelists? Consider a few reasons the local evangelist
is a key to building up the local church.

The Preacher Is the Source

In most congregations, the preacher delivers at least
two sermons a week and teaches at least two Bible
classes—the latter normally to an adult, if not auditorium, class. The fruits of his study provide the number
one source of biblical information the average Christian
receives outside his or her personal study. Therefore, he
must take heed to what he says there (1 Timothy 4:16).

Here are some words of wisdom for the preacher:

- *Do not state opinions as facts.* It is all right, so long as they are harmless, to state opinions. It is certainly all right to present facts. However, never represent one as being the other. Preachers who press others to accept their opinions as gospel divide churches. Study the Bible carefully and craft sermons that really do tell the truth.

- *Do not preach without adequate preparation.* It would be amusing if not so shameful to hear a preacher speak of "winging it" in the pulpit. The saddest part is that he thinks nobody knows, but it is always apparent. My experience is that those who boast proudly of extemporizing are those whose attempts are most obvious. There is no shortcut to preaching a meaty, effective sermon. It requires time, study, and practice: "Be diligent to present yourself approved to God" (2 Timothy 2:15). Does this not include sermon preparation?

- *Do present balanced sermons: rebuke and exhort, comfort and convict, preach hard and soft sermons.* Too much one-sided preaching will make the hearer "whop-sided." Unbalanced preaching can lead the listeners to get "off balanced." From beginning to end, the Bible warns and encourages us to stay on biblical center (Deuteronomy 4:2; Joshua 1:7; Proverbs 30:6; Revelation 22:18–19). My dad's preaching philosophy has always been to "comfort the afflicted and afflict the comfortable." Preachers do well to labor with such a mentality.

- *Do constantly work on improving yourself as a preacher.* The bottom-line goal of preaching and teaching is to relate eternal truths to everyday, practical living. The emphasis of the sermon must be the Bible. Older preachers have often said, "Fill your sermon with Scripture. At least you will know that part of it will be right." The objective of the sermon must be to convince, change, comfort, and call the hearers. The goal of every sermon should not be to "leave 'em feeling good," nor should it be always to "leave 'em feeling guilty." Again, the concept is balance. Then the presentation of the sermon must be adequate. This requires proper preparation and a constant goal of improving the delivery. How often is the Lord insulted by the casual, haphazardous, and careless attitude that comes across in the ill-prepared, poorly presented sermon? Because the honorable preacher is convinced that the message of the Bible, man's salvation through Christ, is the most important subject of them all, he always strives to improve his effectiveness in preaching it.

What the preacher preaches and how he communicates the message profoundly impacts the church, whether it is uplifted or downtrodden. Remember: "Death and life are in the power of the tongue" (Proverbs 18:21). Each preacher must carefully and prayerfully ask, "Is my preaching killing spirits or preserving souls?"

The Preacher Is Closely Watched

That does not mean a preacher should put his family in a fish bowl inside a glass house. It does not mean that the preacher should not be normal. Kept in proper perspective, sports, current events, hobbies, and the like have a needed place in his life. He needs to take adequate time for his family. He needs time away from the job. Nor do I suggest that a preacher lives to cater to his critics. Hypercriticism is no doubt one of the most often cited sources of discouragement with which preachers must contend. It is probable that there will be Christians lost for their merciless hypercriticism of the preacher and his family (James 2:13; Matthew 18:15–17).

Yet, it is an unavoidable fact that the preacher is watched. Members of the community see him around town. Neighbors watch him in his yard. Church members see him various places during the week. Old people and little people notice him. Strangers and acquaintances are watching him. His wife and children see him, too.

The young preacher Timothy was told to watch his example (1 Timothy 4:12). Do not be guilty of unchristian behavior in any setting. Because every preacher should desire to be a faithful Christian, let him dress modestly and appropriately, be "sound in speech, which is beyond reproach" (Titus 2:8), and portray a positive, Christ-like attitude devoid of bitterness (Ephesians 4:31), slandering and insult (1 Peter 3:9), hate (Titus 3:8), and cynicism (1 Timothy 6:4).

The Preacher Is Trusted

Woe to the preacher who violates the trust placed in him by God and man! Being a faithful, gospel preacher includes being trustworthy (1 Thessalonians 2:4). Beware of the following traps that terminate trust:

- Being intimate or indiscreet with a woman other than his wife.
- Being slothful and lazy; robbing God and the church of time that belongs to them.
- Being unethical in business practices.
- Engaging in any sinful habit or form of entertainment.
- Engaging in gossip about church members.
- Causing strife and division, disrupting church harmony.

This list is not exhaustive, but it surely calls to memory ways in which preachers have violated the sacred trust they have as proclaimers of God's Word. The expectations above apply to all members, but as the church's "front man," the preacher's lack of circumspection and discretion in behavior and ethics can be much more damaging than when other members engage in similar behavior.

Drawn to Calvary

Preachers who serve as good role models, who work hard, who show interest in the members—rich or poor, educated or not, or influential or not—who do not forget their families, who are well-rounded and well-adjusted, and who live what they preach help build up the local church in a marvelous way. Young men who watch the local preacher will have a high regard for preaching, and they will want to follow in his footsteps. The lost of the community and non-Christian friends of members will be drawn to Calvary through his godly influence. The members of the congregation where he preaches will be more apt to practice what he preaches. God bless the church universal with more great preachers.

MAKING IT PRACTICAL

- *Congregations should train men to preach.* The curriculum should include courses dealing with basic principles of sermon preparation and delivery. Such training may whet the appetite of those undecided about their choice of careers. It will give the church additional preaching resources for times when the preacher is away or the church is "between preachers."

- *Congregations should let their preachers know how much they are appreciated.* Elders do well who stand up periodically and publicly commend particularly difficult sermons on challenging or unpopular subjects, such as modesty, giving, and instrumental music. The greatest way to communicate appreciation for a preacher's work is by putting the lessons he preaches into practice.

- *Congregations should make a concerted effort to encourage their young men to consider becoming preachers.* If the position of preacher has an honorable place in our eyes, it will in the eyes of the young men. A good preacher role model is particularly needed in our homes for our Christian youth.

- *Congregations should avoid the following "confidence busters" for the preacher.* These items are also extremely disturbing to the faithful:

  Lethargic Singing: Lifeless singing or singing without effort or enthusiasm kills the preacher's momentum as he is preparing to mount the pulpit (1 Corinthians 14:15).

  Talk-a-Thons: Chattering among young folks, conversations of middle-aged folks, and comments between old folks communicates to the preacher a lack of audience interest in God's Word.

  The Fashionably Tardy: Shuffling in at half-past started and half-till over really takes the wind out of the sails of God's messengers.

  The Restroom Rush: Constant popping up, popping out, and popping in effectively disrupts the flow and concentration of the presenter.

The Eyelid Flashers: Those who regularly find their chins in their chests, whose snores impair their neighbors' hearing, and whose unconsciousness draws attention to themselves, assault the proclaimer's enthusiasm.

The Dusty Bibles: Listeners who use their Bibles as armrests, fans, or floor décor convey disinterest to the preacher (Acts 17:11–12).

The Official Timekeepers: The preacher is discouraged by the committee of individuals who could tell him, to the second, how long his sermon was. Some even set their watches for him.

The Songbook Dash: As the preacher sums up his lesson and begins to extend the invitation, nothing cues him in to the inattentiveness and discourtesy of his listeners like the chorus of swishes drowning out his appeals to the lost sinner and wayward lamb.

The Armchair Preacher/Pew Side-Critic: After services, the preacher appreciates nothing like destructive criticism or disagreeable "disagreers." Nothing fails to complement an outpouring of love and concern like the incoming bomb of tongue-lashing (James 3:3–12).

Growing up the son of a preacher, I have seen and heard of many preachers who were always moving in search of a "good local work." Something was always insufficient, usually either salary or soundness. Sometimes these men had either worked with or known of congregations that were spiritually deficient or seemingly without future. Sadly, these congregations do exist. Other times, though, the preachers were restless or idealistic. Preachers should be careful and deliberate before choosing to leave one work for another. Though there are many considerations that might make a new work attractive, be careful. The grass is not always greener on the other side.

QUESTIONS FOR THOUGHT

1. Why is the preacher a dominant force in the personality of a congregation? What are the pros and cons of this widespread reality?

2. What qualities do you think make a preacher effective? What is the scriptural basis for such qualities? Do you think that some expectations are tied more to tradition (what preachers have done) than to the Bible (how God defines his work)? Give examples.

4. How can a congregation evaluate how it is perceived? Why is such an evaluation an important exercise?

5. What common areas would change in members' lives if we had an active, ongoing emphasis on trying to emulate the mind and actions of Christ? In what areas is such an emphasis most needed in the congregation where you worship?

CHAPTER TEN

Encouragement

Plans that Backfire

Have you been discouraged lately? Have you failed at something? Remember a professional's "Grammatical error." Bill Grammatica, that is. The rookie had been having a great first season, faring even better than his older brother, Tampa Bay's Martin Grammatica. Then, against the New York Giants on December 15, 2001, Grammatica became a little over-exuberant about making a field goal. Jumping for joy, he landed awkwardly on one foot and in the process tore his right anterior cruciate ligament (ACL), making that field goal his last for 2001. The Ticker report said, "Bill forever will be entrenched on blooper reels as the kicker who blew out his knee celebrating a field goal." Ouch!

Sometimes we have good intentions, but our plans backfire. Other times, we get hurt in the process of doing something nice for others. Maybe, with honorable intentions, we really foul up things. This can be discouraging and even embarrassing. We can even be tempted to think, "Why bother?"

Maybe it is not a mistake you have made. You may get discouraged because of the actions or the inactions of others. Discouragement can come from just about anywhere. Sometimes you can be discouraged and depressed and not even know why. What a powerful, spiritual fortifying we get from Vitamin "E" (encouragement).

Encouraging and Rebuking

Paul rebuked false teachers and false teaching. He did not compromise the truth of God's Word. He defended the faith and denounced error. Yet in his life and work, the apostle Paul also encouraged, uplifted, and appreciated the good works of his good brethren. He commended often. He was generous in praising and defending his fellow Christians. He had a healthy respect, love, and relationship with numerous children of God throughout his life, as his inspired writings prove.

When Paul wrote to correct a fault, he often named those who were misbehaving and said something good about them. He also praised the faithful by name.

If my calculations are right, about one percent of the verses in Paul's epistles contain the names of those he rebukes. At least two of the nineteen individuals he named were not members of the church. Five percent of the verses in the Pauline epistles contain the names of those Paul commends.

Please understand that Paul constantly rebuked immorality and doctrinal unsoundness. He warned of hell and the judgment to come. He warned that Christianity involves total sacrifice and commitment. He also spoke of heaven, grace, and love divine. And no one in Scripture, apart from Christ, ever refined the art of encouragement as Paul did. The local church must be filled with Christians like Paul, who know how to encourage others.

Encourage the Young

Jesus loved little children (Matthew 18:1–3). The local church without a sizeable share of young people is limited in its hope for the future. That being the case, we must do all we can to encourage them and not ignore them. This does not mean catering to our children so that we spoil them or cause them to lose sight of the preeminence of service. It does mean that we find ways to encourage and interact with them.

- *Provide a vital, viable education program.* Greater detail is given to this in chapter 3, but it cannot be over emphasized. Enthusiastic, well-prepared, and resourceful teachers who emit genuine love for their students greatly encourage these precious little ones.

- *Provide spiritual and service opportunities.* Emphasize that worship and service demand and deserve a more important place in a youth program than entertainment and eating. The latter have their place and value, but times for devotionals, good fellowship activities with other Christian young people, and service projects such as cutting an elderly person's grass, taking food to the poor or shut-ins, or visiting a nursing home should be given higher places.

- *Pay attention to them.* Shake their hands after worship. Take an interest in their lives, their schoolwork, their after-school activities, and their interests. Call them by name. Look for and praise the admirable qualities they possess. Enlist their help in church projects.

Encourage the Elderly

In a society characterized by its glamorization and obsession with the youth movement, but where everyone on average is living longer, Christians in their golden years may find themselves increasingly discouraged. The world may wish to ignore or discard them, but a great local church will not!

- *Visit the elderly.* Those who outlive their mates, friends, and contemporaries get lonely. How many elderly Christians sit alone in nursing homes, assisted-living apartments, or their residences with only memories? Do not forget the elderly! A bouquet of flowers and a thirty-minute visit will live with them a long time. So small an investment for so great a return!

- *Volunteer to help older folks.* As their eyesight fails, their health grows feeble, and they are no longer able to drive or get around as they wish, younger Christians can take senior saints to the grocery store, to doctor visits, or to see a sibling or friend. Human nature does not want to ask for help; take the initiative.

Encourage the Sick

We have all made the joke about the well-meaning but awkwardly stated prayer: "Be with those sick of this congregation." But we understand what it means. Every congregation always has members who suffer illnesses. Members are usually suffering at home from short illnesses such as flu, colds, and the like. Typically there are a number in the hospital with sudden or one-time problems. Then there are the chronically ill. All of these, particularly those whose problems are ongoing, need encouraging. This can be done through calls and cards. When possible, we need to visit. In fact, Jesus makes it imperative for His disciples to visit the sick (Matthew 25:36).[3]

---

3. "Visit" in this verse is from the Greek verb erchomai, found 119 times in Matthew. In Matthew 25, it occurs in some form a total of nine times to speak, either literally or figuratively, of Christ's coming (10, 13, 19, 27, 31). As sure as He will come, we are expected to go to those who are sick and in prison. What, then, of the excuses often made for why we fail to obey the command to visit the "sick among us"?

Depression and despair often accompany debilitations, especially long-term ones. Brotherly empathy will move those "church builders" in a congregation to act upon such feelings (Romans 12:15; Acts 9:37–42).

Encourage the New Christian

A sobering, sometimes overlooked part of the parable of the soils has to do with what happens to those who actually become Christ's disciples. There seems indication from the parallel Gospels that those represented by the rocky soil and thorny soil are disciples who later fall away, not faithfully enduring to the end.[4] All of this means that more mature Christians must pay special care and attention to the newly converted. Under the best of circumstances, living the Christian life is difficult (Acts 14:22; 2 Timothy 3:12; Luke 13:24). Destructive choices made by older Christians not only serve to jeopardize their own souls but can discourage and destroy the faith of new Christians. Christ pronounces a woeful warning against those who so behave (Matthew 18:6). On the other hand, we must take necessary steps to give new Christians special attention and help them grow. Every time they attend services, tell them you are glad to see them. Do not take their decision to come for granted. Involve them in the work of the church. Invite them, along

---

4. Boles, for instance, speaks of those in rocky soil as they who, at first, give the impression that they will make faithful children of God, but they ultimately desert Him. Likewise, the thorny-ground type as being like those "in the church today" (Commentary on Luke, 169–170). Words such as "receive" and "fall away" reinforce the idea of Christians who fall away other than those who reject the Word (8:11) without having made an obedient response to it. See also McGarvey (Matthew and Mark, 119–120), Coffman on Mark (78–79), and even Robertson on Luke (114).

with other Christian families, into your home. Get to know their interests, hobbies, and even the challenges they face.

Encourage the New Member

Did you ever have to move to a new school or relocate to take a job? If so, you already know the trials that come with that. New members come to us from congregations where they were known, trusted, and used in God's service. Moving to a new place means starting at ground zero. Some are adept at implanting themselves into the life and work of the new local church. Others are shy by nature and need encouragement. Take no new member for granted. Assume all are shy and are waiting for you to make the first move.

I remember moving my family into a new subdivision. No one came to welcome us. It took us months to meet our neighbors. That reflects a trend in our modern society, though not a positive one. It is very important that our "community," the local church, does not respond that way to our new "neighbors." Be warm, attentive, and accepting to new members. Practice the *Golden Rule* (Matthew 7:12).

Encourage the Overlooked

We often overlook a sizeable portion of the local church in resounding need of encouragement: faithful Christians who fit into no particular category. This includes singles, widows or widowers, those having undergone major life changes—the divorced, those whose nest has recently emptied, those who become unemployed, and even the average family, as if there is such a family! What about those you can always count on? One brother recently identified himself to me as one of our congregation's many silent soldiers. These work behind the scenes, serving and doing the unglamorous. They need encouraging. Praise them often and publicly. Frequently check on them; ask them how they are doing. No one likes to be taken for granted.

Encourage the Visitor

It takes a lot of courage to walk into a strange auditorium—certainly some are stranger than others! This is true of traveling Christians who stop in to visit. It is especially true of non-Christians who, for one reason or another, elect to visit.

Evangelism is a "go ye" business, but so many times we have golden opportunities with the "come theys." When they come to one of our services, we must let them know we are glad they did. Be enthusiastic! Be genuine! Be interested! Ask visitors' names; listen closely and remember them. Invite them to lunch. Even if the family budget is tight, what a wonderful, spiritual way to spend God's money—and wives and mothers escape kitchen duty for a day. (Remember Luke 6:38.) Where appropriate, make an appointment to visit them in their home that week.[5]

Dale Carnegie once wrote,

> You have it easily in your power to increase the sum total of this world's happiness now. How? By giving a few words of sincere appreciation to someone who is lonely or discouraged. Perhaps you will forget tomorrow the kind words you say today, but the recipient may cherish them over a lifetime.

---

5. Keep in mind that we are to be "wise as serpents and harmless as doves" (Matthew 10:16, emp. NP). If you are genuinely interested in the souls of non-Christians, be wise. Don't come on too strong or bombard them with "too much, too soon." Work first at building a relationship and rapport. This goes much further toward setting a Bible study! And that's the goal, isn't it?

What wisdom! Never forget that! Remember the divine exhortations: "Encourage the fainthearted, help the weak" (1 Thessalonians 5:14). "Therefore, strengthen the hands that are weak and the knees that are feeble, and make straight paths for your feet, so that the limb which is lame may not be put out of joint, but rather be healed" (Hebrews 12:12–13). That will help build up the local church!

THE ART OF ENCOURAGEMENT

Encouragers are not born. They're made!
They want to help and not for some accolade.
They give themselves wholly and generously.
They want to build others up spiritually.

They look for their moments, these holy supporters,
For they think of the Kingdom, its expandable borders.
They want to uplift and prefer one another,
Think not of themselves, but defer to the other.

There is no set limit for how many can do it.
It's simple enough, when you get right down to it.
Just pick out somebody or two, five, or ten.
Encourage them often and times without end.

Making It Practical

- *Consider placing an "Information Center" prominently in your foyer.* Staff it with helpful, friendly members to assist visitors in finding classrooms, restrooms, fellowship areas, and the auditorium. Such assistance is a tangible way to encourage visitors to return.

- *Use your church directory to find and call those who have been absent or those who are going through difficult times.* Keep your conversation brief and positive. Tell your contacts that you love and care about them. Remember Carnegie's remarks. It may live with them for a lifetime.

- *Implement ways of encouraging the various segments of a congregation.* Elders, as shepherds, must take the lead and coordinate this work. They are to know, tend, and care for the sheep. There is no shortcut in this work.

- *Encourage the preacher to bring messages that promote Christian living, and compliment him when he does.* Members come to worship, often fresh off some spiritual battle line. They may be very discouraged when they enter. Sermons that inspire hope, give confidence, and provide motives and methods for successfully coping with discouragement are important to a congregation's spiritual welfare.

- *Start and maintain a card program.* Christian women excel in this work. Those who volunteer can be assigned by the program's coordinator—preferably also a woman—two or three people's names to whom they each in turn send cards. The list of recipients could include shut-ins, the sick, those recently baptized or restored, non-Christian visitors, and Christians who visit from sister congregations. My wife such started a program at a congregation where I preached; the impact was profound.[6]

---

6. We had a Bible correspondence course student who came because he received so many cards. Our associate minister recently said, "The card program is alive and well . . . I received a dozen cards while I was sick." At a wedding I performed not long ago, an elderly Christian couple from Missouri said that several women wrote them when they made a visit and in all their travels had never had a church do that. A multiplied number of stories from members, visitors, and non-Christians could be readily produced. People love being remembered and appreciated!

QUESTIONS FOR THOUGHT

1. When was the last time you stopped to encourage a small child in the congregation (to whom you were not related)? Why is such encouragement so invaluable?

2. Why are we uncomfortable visiting some groups— shut-ins, those in the hospital, or the elderly? What can we do to get past these discomforts and help others to do the same?

3. What can the following groups do to become active encouragers: Introverted? New Christians? Teenagers?

4. How should church leaders incorporate new members into the work of the church? What cautions do you recommend?

5. What is your strongest way of communicating— letters, emails, telephone calls, face-to-face visits? What ways have you found to encourage those who seem the most appreciated? Who in the congregation do you think is particularly good at encouraging? What are the characteristics that make them effective?

CHAPTER ELEVEN

Emulation

Imitate the Admirable

Webster's New World Dictionary maintains one of the better definitions for the word *emulate:* "To try to equal or surpass; to imitate (a person or thing admired), to rival successfully." It is particularly the middle definition we have in mind when we speak of what it takes to build up the local church. We are not trying to compete but rather to complete! Better still, we are trying to be complete. This is our guiding star: "And let endurance have its perfect result, so that you may be perfect and complete, lacking in nothing" (James 1:4).

Who or what admirable model are we trying to imitate? Are there things that we are trying to equal and even surpass? How can such striving and ambition help the local church of which we are members? Consider a few scriptural suggestions for growing up into Christ in all things in the church where we labor (Ephesians 4:15).

Emulate Christ

This is the first and last of any discussion, isn't it? Peter told some struggling saints, "For you have been called for this purpose, since Christ also suffered for you, leaving you an example for you to follow in His steps" (1 Peter 2:21). This text is often rightly cited to prove that we should follow the example of Jesus. Yet to remove it from its context robs it of its meaning to those Christians, that is, to emulate their Redeemer role model.

We should emulate His handling of mistreatment (1 Peter 2:19–23). Christ was mistreated, though He was perfectly innocent. He did not take revenge, though He had the power (Matthew 26:53). Instead, He trusted that the Father would eventually set all things right. What an example! If someone, even another member where you attend, offends or hurts you, Christ has given you the proper channel to handle it (Matthew 18:15–17). Yet, when in the worst of worse-case scenarios, act like Jesus! Certainly, if unbelievers persecute you for your faith, "consider it all joy, my brethren, when you encounter various trials, knowing that the testing of your faith produces endurance" (James 1:2–3).

We should emulate His sinless conduct (1 Peter 2:22). No, we will never be sinless. However, it is incumbent upon us to try. What child who sets out to be a basketball star uses as his example an overweight, out of shape man who cannot hit a single basket (read "Dad")? He looks at the most successful professional basketball player he can find. Then he watches how he shoots, dribbles, and defends.

Just so, if our goal is heaven, we must choose the best example of how to survive this life successfully—Jesus! Wherever we find sin in our lives, we work on eliminating it!

We should emulate His level of sacrifice (1 Peter 2:24). Observe the nature of His sacrifice.

- It was *personal:* "He Himself."
- It was *painful:* "bore our sins in His body."
- It was *purposeful:* "that we might die to sin and live in righteousness."
- It was *precious:* by it we "were healed."

Look at the level of your sacrifice. What are you doing to help the church grow; what are you doing to touch the life of one who needs you? Do you sacrifice at a level that really involves sacrifice—something that hurts to part with for the sake of Christ and His church? Have you purposefully set out to sacrifice, whether in money, talent, or other personal involvement? To determine whether or not you sufficiently sacrifice, examine the tangible results of your involvement in the strengthening and stabilizing of the church where you attend and labor.

Emulate the Right Christian Examples

Lethargic, lazy, inconsistent, non-sacrificial, worldly members may be poor examples, but they sure are easy to follow. They walk the path of least resistance (Matthew 7:13–14). They are not carrying a cross, so their load appears lighter (Luke 9:23). Remember this about wrong examples: If you follow them, and they get into eternal trouble, you stumble right along after them (Luke 17:1–2).

Paul says, "Be imitators of me, just as I also am of Christ" (1 Corinthians 11:1). That is the basic, one-point criteria for determining who should be followed. If they follow Jesus, follow them. How do you know which members are following Jesus?

- *Watch their speech.* Is it pure and wholesome? Is it kind?

- *Watch their attendance.* Do they do whatever they can to be present, or do they use any and every excuse to be absent?

- *Watch their attitude.* Is it winsome and agreeable, or is it cantankerous and obnoxious?

- *Watch their interests.* Are they sensual, shady, and downright sinful, or do they engage in activities that you can join in without fear of Christ's second coming?

The answer to these questions is usually much more elementary and uncomplicated than we might suppose.

Emulate the Right Qualities

Make sure your life adds up. Peter tells us how to do this (2 Peter 1:5–7). Add the right characteristics in the process of your Christian living—from faith to love. Peter encourages us by adding: "For if these qualities are yours and are increasing, they render you neither useless nor unfruitful in the true knowledge of our Lord Jesus Christ" (2 Peter 1:8).

Grow the right fruit. Paul, after presenting an alarming list of spiritual weeds like fornication, outbursts of anger, selfish ambition, drunkenness, and the proverbial "like" sins, tells us what to plant in the garden of our heart: "But the fruit of the Spirit is love, joy, peace, patience, kindness, goodness, faithfulness, gentleness, self-control" (Galatians 5:22–23). We will never regret incorporating any of these attributes. The presence of these traits defines true spirituality.

The Quality that Never Fails

Refine how you are defined. In the midst of his lengthy discussion about miraculous gifts in the early church, Paul emphasizes the important, abiding, and most needful quality in the local church. That quality is love. The Holy Spirit through Paul defines it this way:

> Love is patient, love is kind and is not jealous; love does not brag and is not arrogant, does not act unbecomingly; it does not seek its own, is not provoked, does not take into account a wrong suffered, does not rejoice in unrighteousness, but rejoices with the truth; bears all

things, believes all things, hopes all things, endures all things. Love never fails (1 Corinthians 13:4–8).

One who takes this list and tries to perfect each individual trait will have a lifelong, daily challenge in incorporating them all. Yet churches need to be filled with people trying to emulate the admirable qualities that constitute love and build up the local church.

A State of Becoming

Christians should engage themselves in a continual routine of self-improvement. Someone said, "Christianity is not a state of being. It is a state of becoming." Each day you live, what are you becoming? Are you becoming more like Jesus? Have you chosen the proper role models to help you reach that goal? What personal qualities are you adding, growing, and refining to help you become the best Christian you can be? By regularly asking these questions and laboring to answer them with an upright life, you will help to build up the church of which you are a member.

Two Prayers in the Temple

Up high and proud my boasts I declare.
I brag and I crow with my head in the air,
Till I look in the corner and see him down there.
Why is that poor sinner locked up in despair?

I abstain from eating two days every week.
I give money too freely, Thy thanks I now seek.
Why is that man crying? The tears stain his cheek.
He's beating his chest, must be some kind of trick.

Lord, I'm not like the swindler, philanderer, or cheat,
Or even like the tax collector with whose prayer I compete.
I'm walking out now, Lord, my preening complete,
But I'll see You here next time my boasts to repeat.

While scarcely detected, a man whispered his plea,
His face to the floor, if not on one bended knee.
All the sinner could say was, "Have mercy on me."
And he left justified, not the proud Pharisee.

MAKING IT PRACTICAL

- *Pick out a person or family in the congregation that you recognize for their faithfulness.* Keeping in mind that no one is perfect—and even the members of your selected family will have shortcomings—watch how they conduct themselves with other Christians, with the lost, and with each other. Take note of the qualities they possess and which you know you should follow. This is a practical way to do what Paul said in 1 Corinthians 11:1.

- *Read through the Gospels and write down each quality of Jesus' personal life revealed by Matthew, Mark, Luke, and John.* For an example, consider Mark 2. Jesus was a discerner of others' faith (v. 5). He helped others how He could (v. 11). He taught others (v. 13). He was a soul winner (v. 14). He was unprejudiced (vv. 15–17). He knew the Scriptures (vv. 25–28). Find other qualities in Mark 2, as well as the remaining eighty-eight chapters of the four books.

Consider the following comparison:

How Sour Attitudes Are Made

A brasiveness—Keep a chip on your shoulder.
T emperamentality—Stay irritable, sensitive, and moody.
T alebearing—Talk bad about others.
I gnorance—Fail to appreciate how God has blessed you.
T emptation—Don't resist, overcome, or avoid it.
U nfaithfulness—Live by the gospel according to self.
D emanding—Expect more than others can do.
E gotism—Put self first.

How Proper Attitudes Are Made

A ction—Do right (Hebrews 5:9; James 1:22).
T houghtfulness—Consider others (Philippians 2:3–4).
T hankfulness—Appreciate blessings (Colossians 3:15).
I deals—Pursue spiritual things (Colossians 3:1–2).
T ests—Overcome trials (James 1:5–6, 12).
U nderstanding—Know how to navigate life (Proverbs 3:5).
D eath—Crucify self (Romans 6:6; Colossians 3:5).
E rasers—Forget past failures (Philippians 3:13).

QUESTIONS FOR THOUGHT

1. Why do new and weak Christians sometimes emulate poorer Christian role models? How can we break this cycle?

2. Someone is always watching you. Why is that so sobering? Who do you think is watching you? Who would you be surprised to know is watching you?

3. What are your greatest strengths as perceived by others? Weaknesses? What are in fact your greatest strengths and weaknesses? How does the list made by others differ from the one made by you? Why?

4. Why is it important for a congregation to evaluate others' perception of it? Why is knowing how we are perceived important?

5. What common areas would change in members' lives if there were an active, ongoing emphasis emulating the mind and actions of Christ? Where this emphasis is most needed?

CHAPTER TWELVE

Expectation

Raise the Goals!

What started as a game for the eventual boys' state championship basketball team became a symbolic ritual. After every grueling practice, the coach would go to the utility closet and press the button that automatically raised the goals up into the gymnasium rafters. Then all the tired boys would take basketballs from the rack and toss them toward the rising hoops. Thunderous cheers followed every made basket. Curious, the coach one day asked the boys, "Why do you boys shoot at those baskets when I take them up?" One of the team captains smiled and replied, "Aw, coach, anybody can hit the goals when they're lowered, but champions hit them when they're raised!"

The future of any congregation can be somewhat determined by the heights of its goals and plans. Where does it hope to be? What does it hope to do? Expectations are an inseparable part of those churches that thrive, grow, and develop into beacons that shine into the lost communities around them. The writer of Hebrews was inspired to say, "Now faith is the assurance of things hoped for, the conviction of things not seen" (Hebrews 11:1). Each individual member of the Lord's church is helping to build a certain destiny in the unseen, unknown place called tomorrow. How can each Christian help build up the church of which he or she is a member?

Expect Growth

How wonderful to hear Christians who say not "if we grow" but rather "as we grow." The first-century church looked at numerical and spiritual growth as the natural end result of their laboring in the kingdom (1 Corinthians 15:58). Despite persecutions, they held dearly their living hope (1 Peter 1:3). From Pentecost on throughout Acts, the church grew (Acts 2:41; 4:4; 6:1, 7; 11:21; 16:5). Yet members did not merely watch its growth; they participated in the process. Expectations were mixed with exertion, anticipation was matched by attempt, and wishes were mingled with working. If Christians in all phases of the work endeavor to "fulfill the law of Christ" (Galatians 6:2), they should expect growth. God wants it, Christians can accomplish it, lost souls depend upon it, and a bright future is contingent upon it. Expect growth!

Anticipate Setbacks

Along with the victories of conversion, restoration, and participation will come disappointments. Christians fall away, brethren offend by word and deed, families cease from active duty, and Bible studies "fall through." Satan is trying hard to stem the tide of any good work (1 Peter 5:8). The world thinks Christian living strange (1 Peter 4:4), so naturally some will reject the message of sanctification (1 Thessalonians 4:3–5). However, God's people should memorize Paul's exhortation: "Let us not lose heart in doing good, for in due time we will reap if we do not grow weary" (Galatians 6:9).

A poem speaks beautifully of a place all saints hope one day to call home:

LONG FOR "HOME"

I wandered from the city
With its noise and dusty streets,
And walked out in the country
Where the air was pure and sweet;

And as I looked around me,
'Twas in the early morn,
Across the hill I saw then
A farmer plowing corn.

It seemed that in an instant
The scene changed to long ago,
And I, a little child again,
Was following the row.

As I often did behind my dad;
We must hoe the corn "just so,"
And if we did, dad always said:
"You may rest at the end of the row."

I see it now, the same old field,
Dad sweating at the plow;
We children following with our hoes,
With him to show us how.

And he always said: "Now do it right
And cut the weeds as you go."
And if we did what father said,
We could rest at the end of the row.

The years have flown, we children grown,
And father is here no more.
But now I gaze on that field of corn
Like we hoed in the days of yore,

And compare this life to that field of corn
As we toil here below.
For Father has said if we do our work right,
We shall rest at the end of the row.
       —Author Unknown

Work toward Heaven

What characterizes a congregation that is on its way home?

- They keep their hands to the plow (Luke 9:62).
- They keep their backs to the world (James 4:4).
- They keep their eyes upon the unseen prize (2 Corinthians 4:18).
- They keep their hearts in the Scriptures (Psalm 119:11).
- They keep their feet on the narrow path (Matthew 7:14).
- They keep their mouths under control (James 3:2–5).
- They keep their knees bent in prayer (Ephesians 3:14).
- They keep their Head (Christ) in control of the body (Colossians 1:18).

Churches that think about, talk about, and work toward heaven not only get there but also grow here.

As Whittier wrote,

> Behind the cloud the starlight lurks,
> through showers the sunbeams fall;
> For God, who loveth all His works,
> has left His hope for all.

How grand to be a part of a church, despite past victories, that can say with full integrity, "The best is yet to be!" With Christ, the end of a thing is far better than the beginning thereof! (Ecclesiastes 7:8).

NEVER TOO LATE TO FOLLOW GOD

> Your eyes may be cloudy,
> A halt may slow your gait,
> But as long as your soul is within you,
> It is never, no never, too late.

The years you may have wasted,
And in shame you might hesitate,
But though it be the "eleventh hour,"
It is never, no never, too late.

MAKING IT PRACTICAL

It is absolutely vital for a church to set goals and plans if it wishes to grow. When a church stops planning, it will lose direction, momentum, and members.

- *Have annual planning sessions.* Use the time not only to verbalize lofty dreams but also to address neglected and needed tasks. Elders who will lead in wisdom realize that the congregation is filled with great ideas waiting to be shared. Some of a church's greatest works began as a point on a wipe board or a bullet in a PowerPoint presentation. Find a place away from the church building—and its attending distractions, such as telephones and members who are not attending the session popping in and out—and a time on the calendar, perhaps as the time for the annual budget approaches.

- *Set "Goal Days" often.* Special attendance drives, "Bring a Friend" day, and "Come Home" Sundays that encourage fallen members to return can provide a spark for the congregation. Develop themes that are challenging but not ridiculous. Goal days encourage members to work more actively toward getting their friends and loved ones "in the building."

- *Think often about heaven.* Try to avoid seeing the eternal abode abstractly. Read great texts that speak of heaven, like Revelation 21–22. Think about personally living eternally in heaven. Positive mental grasp of eternal life will prove a powerful motivator and an inoculation against the disease of discouragement.

Expect some of your fellow Christians to "cop out" of the work. Flimsy excuses almost always accompany "cop out" announcements. I am reminded of a Christian lady who asked her neighbor to attend a gospel meeting. The neighbor responded by saying that he and his wife could not attend church because of her allergies! Apparently, the perfumes of those attending so bothered her that she could not go to the house of worship. He conceded the awfulness of her situation but was confident God would overlook their lack of attendance. The same sister, who knows and loves this couple, had bumped into her sneezy neighbor countless times in the store. The couple celebrated their fiftieth anniversary with a party hosted in their home. Many guests attended, most of whom also attended church somewhere. The sister also attended and sorrowfully reported that almost every guest wore perfume. Fortunately, this neighbor survived the party.

Few excuses surpass getting sick from church, but some of the excuses Christians give—while being more trite—are equally flimsy. If these excuses cannot survive the scrutiny of the Savior at the judgment, those giving them will not survive the judgment. Yet, while living here below and laboring in the kingdom, may Christians who endure such excuses from their brethren not lose heart!

QUESTIONS FOR THOUGHT

1. Do you think the congregation you now attend will be larger, smaller, or the same size in ten years? What can the congregation do now to influence that answer in a positive way?

2. What is most valuable about having regular planning sessions or vision meetings?

3. What common things discourage growth and planning? Who is most responsible for encouraging high expectations? Why?

4. How did the first-century church, though often persecuted and challenged by false teaching and internal immorality, manage to maintain such lofty goals and reach for great expectations?

5. How does thinking about heaven adjust our expectations for the church, for others, and, most importantly, for ourselves?

CHAPTER THIRTEEN

Epilogue

Many qualities not addressed in this work will help build up congregations. The church must constantly stay in a "building program," not the building of structures but of souls. No cliché is more traveled among gospel preachers than this one: "There is no perfect church just as there is no perfect preacher." Every local church will have its attending strengths and weaknesses. By way of summary, consider some qualities that will encourage us to become stronger—more viable lighthouses, salt-shakers, hospitals, armies, and families.

- *An Evangelistic Membership.* How many Christian brothers and sisters are trained, experienced, and desirous of doing personal evangelism, taking seriously the Lord's *Great Commission?* (Matthew 28:18–20). Is the congregation receptive to studies with people of all races, social climes, and educational backgrounds? Do they see the world as a harvest in which they must labor? (Matthew 9:37).

- *A Spiritual Leadership.* Elders are not perfect men (Romans 3:23). Every elder is stronger in some areas than others. Yet, look at the eldership's thrust. Are the men interested in spiritual matters? Are they visiting, encouraging, disciplining, caring, praying, studying, teaching, evangelizing, delegating, trusting, vigilant men? Is their time spent more in financial concerns or spiritual concerns? Do they support balanced, gospel preaching? Are they safe examples to follow?

- *A Caring Fellowship.* Observe the secret acts of charity and love. Many Christian families regularly, though usually anonymously, buy groceries for families in need, buy presents during the holidays for children who otherwise would not have much, take food to the sick or hurting, make visits, write cards, and make phone calls to those suffering and shut in. Such actions serve as gauges of a people making an effort to please God and imitate Christ.

- Further, notice how they accept new converts and include Christians in their fellowship who have recently moved into their community. Although not in spiritual fellowship with them, notice how they treat non-Christian visitors to the assembly? Is there a sense that the brethren are letting "love of the brethren continue" (Hebrews 13:1), despite the common strains and disagreements that can test a congregation? This is significant.

- *An Effective Pulpit.* Certainly, this does not necessarily mean flowery, dynamic, or bubbly. Preachers have "bad days on the job," experience discouragement ("blue days"), and suffer disappointments by the actions of brethren. They may on occasion say something unwise or tactless—privately or from the pulpit—but certainly this should not regularly characterize God's preacher. When every day is sour, discouragement cannot be defeated. Bitterness, always visible, is detrimental to the membership. When no sermon is complete without mentioning a certain subject, the work quickly ceases to be "a good one." And when the pulpit stays silent on a "hard subject" in interest of job security, caters to the feelings of a specific segment of the brethren, or either implicitly or explicitly spreads false teaching, the work of that church ceases to be a good work directly because of an ineffective pulpit.

There will be bad days, hurt feelings, disappointing behavior, stressful situations, apathy, resistance, and heartaches in the best of congregations. The membership, the leadership, and the fellowship will falter. So will the pulpit. Yet patience in teaching and growing can brighten the perspective. May every local church, every member included, cooperate to make the work a good one in God's eyes!

QUESTIONS FOR THOUGHT

1. What would you add to this list of sundry qualities that will help the church to grow?

2. Of all the areas addressed, who or what is most important to the success of the church's growth? Who or what is the least important?

3. What value can be derived from church growth books written by those who are not members of the Lord's church? Aside from false teaching on church growth or other biblical subjects, what other cautions should be heeded when consulting these?

4. How can churches cope with growth slumps or declining numbers? What are some things they should not do?

5. What elements should be considered when planning for growth in the congregation? (Consider such matters as building location, program emphasis, missions, and evangelism.)

Additional Resources

There has been a flurry of books in recent years on church growth, especially from enthusiastic and bright men, nonetheless in religious error. Some of these books are of greater depth and substance than others. All of them contain varying degrees of terminological and theological shortcomings. They use words like "witnessing," refer to the preacher as "pastor," and include in their idea of legalism those who oppose mechanical instrumental music in worship. This is only a small sampling of the kinds of things the alert reader will uncover in the course of reading them. Being aware of these problem areas, one will be surprised at the number of good ideas and concepts which, interpreted with a proper biblical hermeneutic, can greatly aid church leaders in planning and plotting for growth. These books address varying components of church growth that we have attempted to explore in this work.

God's people face two choices: to try to grow or not try to grow. The latter is not a viable choice for a congregation of God's people. It disconnects them from the first-century church that grew and grew despite adversities and limitations. A church may try without success, but it will not succeed in pleasing God without constantly trying to grow. With that grain of salt before you, read cautiously and keenly books like those listed below to help you build up the church.

Barna, George. *Grow Your Church from the Outside: Understanding the Unchurched and How to Reach Them.* Ventura, CA: Regal Books, 2002.

Colson, Charles and Ellen Vaughn. *Being the Body: A New Call for the Church to Be Light in the Darkness.* Nashville: W Publishing Group, 2003.

Cymbala, Jim. *Fresh Power: Experiencing the Vast Resources of the Spirit of God.* Grand Rapids, MI: Zondervan, 2001.

Hughes, R. Kent. Set Apart: *Calling a Worldly Church to a Godly Life.* Wheaton, IL: Good News Pub., 2003.

Lewis, Robert with Rob Wilkins. *The Church of Irresistible Influence: Bridge-Building Stories to Help Reach Your Community.* Grand Rapids, MI: Zondervan, 2001.

McIntosh, Gary L. *Biblical Church Growth: How You Can Work with God to Build a Faithful Church.* Grand Rapids, MI: Baker Books, 2003.

Ogden, Greg. *Transforming Discipleship: Making Disciples a Few at a Time.* Downers Grove, IL: Intervarsity Press, 2003.

Pope, Randy. *The Prevailing Church: An Alternative Approach to Ministry.* Chicago: Moody Press, 2002.

Rainer, Thom. *Surprising Insights from the Unchurched: and Proven Ways to Reach Them.* Grand Rapids: Zondervan, 2001.

Russell, Bob. *When God Builds a Church: 10 Principles for Growing a Dynamic Church.* West Monroe, LA: Howard Publishing Co., 2000.

Strauch, Alexander. *Biblical Eldership: An Urgent Call to Restore Biblical Church Leadership.* Littleton, CO: Lewis & Roth Pub., 1995.

Toler, Stan. *The Vibrant Church: A Step-By-Step Plan for Bringing Your Church to Life.* Kansas City: Beacon Hill Press, 2002.

Towns, Elmer and Douglas Porter. *Churches That Multiply: A Bible Study of Church Planting.* Kansas City: Beacon Hill Press, 2003.

END NOTES

H. Leo Boles, *Commentary on the Gospel by Luke* (Nashville, TN: Gospel Advocate Company, 1950).

James Burton Coffman, *Commentary on Mark* (Austin TX: Firm Foundation Publishing House, 1975).

J. W. McGarvey, *A Commentary on Matthew and Mark* (Vol. I) (Delight AR: Gospel Light Publishing Company, 1875).

Archibald Thomas Robertson, *Word Pictures in the New Testament* (Vol. II) (Nashville TN: Broadman Press, 1930).

J. J. Turner, *Christian Leadership Handbook: How to Be Worth Following* (West Monroe, LA: Howard Publishing Company, 1991).

Wendell Winkler, *Leadership: The Crisis of Our Time* (Tuscaloosa, AL: Winkler Publications, Inc.). *Leadership: The Crisis of Our Time,* and the others in the series can be ordered from: Winkler Publications, Inc., 2704 Battlement Dr. N.E., Tuscaloosa, Alabama 35406.